NOAH BORRERO & SHAWN BIRD

Closing the Achievement Gap

How to Pinpoint Student Strengths to Differentiate Instruction and Help Your Striving Readers Succeed

D1636856

SCHOLASTIC

New York • Toronto • London • Auckland • Sydney
Mexico City • New Delhi • Hong Kong • Buenos Aires

Credits

The author and the publisher wish to thank those who have generously given permission to use borrowed material: Page, 80, "My Papa's Waltz" Copyright © 1942 by Hearst Magazines, Inc. from COLLECTED POEMS OF THEODORE ROETHKE by Theodore Roethke. Used by permission of Doubleday, a division of Random House, Inc.;
Page 120, "Cancer patient had salmonella prior to death" by Allan Turner. Houston Chronicle.

Scholastic Inc. grants teachers permission to photocopy the reproducible pages of this book for classroom use only. No other part of this publication may be reproduced in whole or in part, or stored in a retrieval system, or transmitted in any form or by any means, electronic, mechanical, photocopying, recording, or otherwise, without written permission of the publisher. For information regarding permission, write to Scholastic Inc., 557 Broadway, New York, NY 10012. .

Editor: Lois Bridges
Production management: Amy Rowe
Cover design: Maria Lilja
Interior design: Holly Grundon
Copy editor: Ilise Weiner
ISBN-13: 978-0-545-04876-7
ISBN-10: 0-545-04876-1
Copyright © 2009 by Noah Borrero and Shawn Bird

All rights reserved. Published by Scholastic Inc.
Printed in the U.S.A.
1 2 3 4 5 6 7 8 9 10   23   15 14 13 12 11 10 09

Table of **Contents**

Part 1: Foundational Understandings

Part 2: Essential Reading Strategies

Part 3: Closing Thoughts

Dedication

To our students—thank you for teaching us.

To our teachers—thank you for loving learning.

Acknowledgments

Writing a book is hard work and would not be possible without the support of many people. We thank the teachers and students who allowed us to come into their classrooms and observe and ask questions. We would like to thank especially Sharon Sharadin for talking about her teaching so honestly and inviting us into her classroom at any time. We would also like to thank the Spring Branch Independent School District for providing Shawn with the freedom to be an instructional leader and to do what is best for students. We greatly appreciate folks at Aspire Public Schools for their access to classrooms, support of this project, and amazing work that they do with students.

No book is written without sacrificing time with family and friends. Thank you for being patient and understanding when we had to skip play in favor of our work on the book. Thank you for sharing your expertise with us, and for always being there to listen.

We have been fortunate throughout this process to work with amazing editors—Lois Bridges and Gloria Pipkin—and a patient production manager, Amy Rowe. Thank you all for your guidance and motivation to see this project through.

Several years ago, Shawn had the great fortune of meeting Cris Tovani when she was hired to consult on content area literacy in the district. Over the years, we have been fortunate to continue working with and learning from her, and we are so fortunate to call her our friend. Our professional association continues today as she comes to our school to work with teachers and help them understand that literacy is the cornerstone of all learning. Thank you, Cris, for your encouragement, but most of all, thank you for what you do each day for kids from all backgrounds and learning abilities. You push us all to continue learning and growing and, because of you, we continually re-think and revise our approach to literacy.

Foreword

Glancing at my morning coffee, I am struck by the quote on the side of the cup. It reads, "People need to see that far from being an obstacle, the world's diversity of languages, religions, and traditions is a great treasure affording us precious opportunities to recognize ourselves in others"(Youssou N'Dour, 2007). Later in the day, I find myself observing a classroom. Amazed by the number of second and third language learners in the class, I walk out with a few of the kids whose native language isn't English and strike up a conversation. Curious to learn more about them, I ask where they are from and what languages other than English they speak. Niema tells me her heritage language is Somali, but she also speaks Arabic. Not to be outdone, Fatima says she is Russian and knows Turkish and Azerbaijani. Satia speaks Swahili but is also learning French. Surrounded by these vibrant voices, I experience a living, breathing example of Youssou N'Dour's quote.

Although it's clear that people who speak multiple languages are powerful learners, educators and administrators may lose sight of this fact as they face intense pressure to close the "achievement gap" immediately. The needs of English language learners are different from those of striving readers. Often I feel inadequate meeting their literacy needs because I haven't been trained as an ESL teacher. I empathize with colleagues who ask me for help because I, too, find myself searching for resources.

Fortunately, when we invite learning, the world has a way of teaching us. For those of us longing to do a better job, help is here. In *Closing the Achievement Gap*, Shawn Bird and Noah Borrero explain how best to support English language learners. They artfully embed snippets of research with real classroom anecdotes, helping readers reshape long-held instructional beliefs.

It is no wonder that many classroom teachers feel inadequate when it comes to meeting the unique and often pressing needs of multi-language learners. ELLs may feel isolated and, therefore, experience immense pressure to assimilate. They are expected to master both a new language and a slate of academic standards in a short period of time. They may also feel inadequate and frustrated as they attempt to share with others what they know and need to learn. Fortunately, readers will find in this book authentic strategies and activities that are culturally responsive and effective for all learners at any ability level. Shawn and Noah's ideas are easy to implement and most importantly, they help students access information. For ELLs, accessing information isn't a choice; it is vital for their survival. As educators we know that literacy enables students to thrive as productive citizens. I think about former ELL students I've taught who tried to sit in the back of the classroom, hoping no one would ask them to speak. After reading *Closing the Achievement Gap*, I feel empowered to invite the ELLs at the back of the room to move up to the center where interactive learning takes place.

Embodying the wise words of Youssou N'Dour, Shawn and Noah help us understand and celebrate diversity as an advantage that we can build on as we strive to close the achievement gaps in our classrooms. The book you are holding, packed with useful background knowledge, is a terrific resource that will improve instruction regardless of student levels. You will gain insight and come to understand how to more effectively meet the needs of ELLs. Believing in one's own teaching ability engenders confidence in students so that they, too, believe they can be successful.

Far from being something to "fix," multilingual learners are a group we should emulate. They provide a window not only to the world but also to a greater understanding of ourselves. In the long run, the people who can read, write, and speak more than one language are uniquely powerful learners who will be the ultimate winners.

—Cris Tovani

Calling All Teachers
To Close the
Achievement Gap

O ur public schools are changing. New students, new teachers, and new administrators fill classrooms and campuses across the nation, and as America's population reaches new heights, so grows the diversity of its citizens.

Schools across the country continue to open their doors to students with culturally, economically, ethnically, and linguistically divergent backgrounds. California, Florida, New York, and Texas continue to be the common entry points for immigrants, but a recently released report commissioned by the Carnegie Corporation titled "Double the Work: Challenges and Solutions to Acquiring Language and Academic Literacy for Adolescent English Language Learners" indicates that the immigrant population has increased in many states across the country, and this part of the population has grown by 200% nationwide from 1993 to 2003 (Short & Fitzsimmons, 2007, p.7).

On the Rise: Immigration at a Glance	
35.2 Million	Immigrants (documented and undocumented) live in the U.S. in 2005
7.9 Million	New immigrants (documented and undocumented) settle in the U.S. between 2000-2005
3.7 Million	Estimated undocumented immigrants settle in the U.S. between 2000-2005
10.3 Million	School-age children come from immigrant families in 2005
12.1%	U.S. population made up of immigrants
18.4%	Immigrants and their U.S.-born children at or below the poverty line

Source: Camerota (2005).

What's more, adding to the challenge of recent arrivals who often have few economic options, many students in our public schools today speak languages other than English at home and are in the process of learning English (Crawford & Krashen, 2007). Spanish is certainly the most common language that students speak at home, but the truth is that students bring many languages to school. The table below shows the most prominent languages that students report speaking at home.

Prominent Second Languages in Today's Schools		
Spanish	Arabic	Kru, Ibo, Uruba
French	Polish	Armenian
Chinese	Japanese	Mon-Khmer, Cambodian
German	Hindi	Hmong
Tagalog	Cantonese	French-Creole
Vietnamese	Persian	Hebrew
Italian	Urdu	
Korean	Mandarin	
	Gujarathi	

Source: Modern Language Association (2005).

Short and Echevarria (2005) note that, "Each year, the United States becomes more ethnically and linguistically diverse. Schools mirror this trend: students from non–English speaking backgrounds represent the fastest growing subset of the K–12 population" (9).

Added to this element of linguistic diversity are the demands of an ever-changing, technologically advanced society. Teenagers in today's world are perhaps more likely to communicate by methods many educators consider "unconventional." Visit any middle or high school campus today and you will find adolescents sending text messages on their cell phones, listening to music, and watching videos on their iPods. While adolescents are skilled at using technology to communicate, teachers are often puzzled by their lack of ability to communicate in "school appropriate" ways. Even as adults, we often ignore traditional grammar rules when sending text messages or e-mails. So, it's no surprise that teenagers prefer to communicate using simplified language. Unfortunately, it is sometimes difficult to help our students break the bad habits that they pick up while using these new communication tools. Many teachers have seen formal essays with shorthand only reserved for text messaging.

As we are faced with the reality of an increasingly complex culture and diverse student population, we must strive to meet the new demands placed on us so that we can give our students a competitive edge as they enter post-secondary education and the global workforce. Data shows that many students do receive an adequate K–12 education and go on to succeed in higher education. Unfortunately, most of the students who do not are often ethnic minorities from low socioeconomic backgrounds (Darling-Hammond, 2007). The disparity in academic achievement between Caucasian students and students of color is stark, and we all recognize the urgent need to close this troubling gap in achievement.

If all of our students are to enjoy successful lives, they must do better academically than the reports from higher education institutions and the national assessment data suggest they do. For example, Trelease (2001) states, "Only 37 percent of high school students score high enough on reading achievement tests to handle adequately college-level material—yet almost 70 percent attempt college. Eighty percent of college faculty members report that entering freshman cannot read well enough to do college work" (p. xiii). This trend cannot continue.

Closing the Achievement Gap

Even more troubling are the data released from the U.S. Department of Education regarding the National Assessment of Educational Progress (NAEP), which is given to fourth, eighth, and twelfth graders across the country. Campbell, Hombo, and Mazzeo (2000) make the following observations from the data: "17 year olds' . . . average [reading] scores from 1984 to 1992 were higher than in 1971. The slight increase between 1971 and 1999, however, was not statistically significant." These data are alarming because they indicate that over three decades, reading achievement among adolescents has remained static. Moreover, the US Department of Education (2003) released "The Nation's Report Card: Reading 2002", which indicates, "The percentages of twelfth graders at or above the *Basic* or *Proficient* levels fell below levels seen in 1992 and 1998" (p. 1). We must reverse these trends.

Certainly, the onus for change is not on teachers alone, but teachers are in the classroom to help their students learn and they need effective strategies that build confidence and foster success.

Teachers in this country are overworked, underpaid, and now under intense scrutiny in every state of the union as high-stakes testing and teacher accountability are at the forefront of national policy (Darling-Hammond, 2007). Certainly, the onus for change is not on teachers alone, but teachers are in the classroom to help their students learn and they need effective strategies that build confidence and foster success. Teachers never intentionally leave children behind; indeed, they are constantly looking for ways to correct the disparity in achievement levels. So, given the demands of teaching adolescents who are growing up with varying world views, the challenges of working with students from many different backgrounds, and the difficulty of helping students who are not proficient in English, what are you, the classroom teacher, to do?

Fortunately, the research findings are clear: successful, confident readers are successful, confident learners (Alfassi, 2004; Beers, 2003; Tovani, 2004; Vacca & Vacca, 2005; Wilhelm, Baker, & Dube, 2001). In sum, those who read, succeed. This then is the aim of our book: to focus on effective reading instruction and to provide you with research-based, targeted reading strategies that will help your students become engaged, strategic readers who not only know *how* to read but *do* read—students who are driven by a quest for information as well as by the sheer desire of getting lost in a good book.

We acknowledge that you, as a secondary teacher, have likely received minimal training in the methods of teaching reading because reading is generally regarded as a skill taught only at the elementary school level. The reality, however, is that our diverse student population requires ongoing instruction in reading. And English Language Learners (ELLs) are not the only students who will benefit from this ongoing instruction. Indeed, any of us could be labeled as a struggling reader. For example, we are professors of education and we feel comfortable reading educational research, but if we were asked to read and comment on a study published in a journal for physicists, we would instantly become struggling readers!

Before we address specific reading strategies, we will use Chapters 1, 2, and 3 to highlight the three essential approaches that we believe are foundational:

❖ building on students' assets

❖ differentiating instruction

❖ facilitating cooperative learning

While some argue that diverse classrooms typically produce lower achievement scores, we believe that diversity strengthens a classroom, creating opportunities for rich conversations and productive peer interaction to encourage higher achievement. Chapter 1 explains both the necessity and promise of building on student strengths. When we shift from a focus on the linguistic deficiencies of ELLs, we discover these students' talents and the great learning advantages they can claim as speakers of more than one language. In Chapter 2, we discuss differentiated instruction as a foundational approach to working with heterogeneous groups of students, and in Chapter 3 we address the many benefits of grouping students for collaborative work.

Chapters 4 through 7 explore specific reading strategies for secondary teachers working with struggling readers in classrooms comprising diverse learners. Each chapter includes "The View From a Classroom" in which a teacher is modeling a particular strategy. These teachers are our colleagues in secondary schools in California and Texas, and they all reveal their beliefs in their students as creative, competent learners. While these teachers come from different grade levels and content areas, and work with different groups of students, they all demonstrate exemplary teaching.

> *Each chapter includes "The View From a Classroom" in which a teacher is modeling a particular strategy.*

Chapter 4 begins our presentation of reading strategies with a focus on pre-reading. We explore Text Preview and Vocabulary Grids as two strategies that all teachers can use to set their students up for success prior to reading a given text. These strategies are simple yet powerful ways of priming students' background knowledge and teaching them to utilize all the information available to them when they encounter different texts.

In Chapter 5 we present perhaps the most powerful strategies a teacher can employ in any classroom, regardless of the content area: interactive read-alouds and monitored sustained silent reading. In his book *The Power of Reading: Insights From the Research*, 2nd Edition, Krashen (2004) reviews relevant research that removes any doubt about the power of independent reading programs in which student choice is a key component. The research will come alive for you when you hear from other teachers who are successfully employing these strategies and noticing the benefits for their students.

"The View From a Classroom" section in Chapter 6 showcases a teacher working on during-reading strategies and post-reading strategies together in one lesson. The *read-aloud, write-aloud* is described as a way to get your students to think about reading as writers, and to improve comprehension by encouraging them to think critically about what they read.

Chapter 7 highlights the important role that questioning plays in students' reading development. Through a glimpse into Ms. Lee's seventh grade science classroom in Houston, Texas, present a strategy that encourages students to make questioning a purposeful part of their routines while they read on their own. We also explain the benefits of Three Part Questioning (3PQ) across content in secondary classrooms.

Chapter 8 is a call for teachers to acknowledge their strengths and the strengths of their students to enhance reading instruction in their classrooms. Let us recognize and embrace two essential understandings: (1) student diversity is an asset, and (2) all students have something to contribute.

It is our aim to equip you with a variety of effective, research-based reading strategies that you can employ confidently, and with that knowledge bring all of your students success. We hope that the foundational research and theory, teaching models, and detailed strategies and tips we provide will make this book an invaluable resource for you as you bring effective instruction to life in your classroom and work to close the achievement gap in your school and community.

Part 1

Foundational Understandings

In order to change academic failure to success, appropriate social and instructional interventions need to occur. For teachers, this means that they need to first acknowledge students' differences and then act as a bridge between their students' differences and the culture of the dominant society . . . That is, they accept and validate the cultural symbols used by all their students.

—Nieto (2002, p. 18)

Chapter 1

AN ASSET APPROACH:
Focus on What Your Kids *Can* Do

In this chapter we strive to make one key point: student diversity should be viewed as an asset and we must embrace and foster this rather than try to "fix" our students. The diversity of the student population in today's public schools is remarkable. Our classrooms are filled with young people from all over the globe, and their instant access to media of all sorts creates challenges for the classroom teacher; of particular concern is the achievement gap between

In this interactive read-aloud, the teacher invites students to follow along in the text as she reads. At certain points in the text, she asks students guiding questions and they record notes, which they refer to in a group discussion that follows the read-aloud.

Caucasian students and students of color. Periodically, the government gives the National Assessment of Educational Progress in reading and math. The results of this test provide a snapshot of the health of the public education system in the United States. Figures 1 and 2 illustrate the achievement gap that exists between Caucasian students and students of color.

Figure 1: The Achievement Gap: 2005 National Reading Scores (Caucasian & African American).

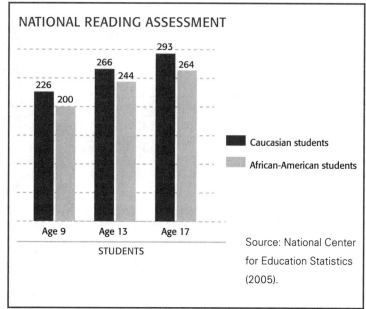

NATIONAL READING ASSESSMENT

Age 9: 226, 200
Age 13: 266, 244
Age 17: 293, 264

Caucasian students
African-American students

STUDENTS

Source: National Center for Education Statistics (2005).

Figure 2: The Achievement Gap: 2005 National Reading Scores (Caucasian & Hispanic).

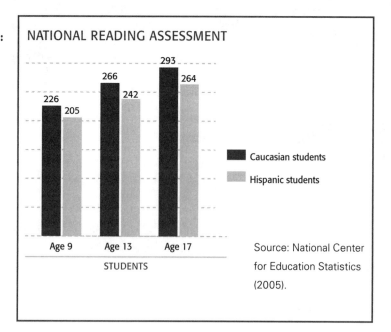

NATIONAL READING ASSESSMENT

Age 9: 226, 205
Age 13: 266, 242
Age 17: 293, 264

Caucasian students
Hispanic students

STUDENTS

Source: National Center for Education Statistics (2005).

Closing the Achievement Gap

The fact that increasing numbers of students who speak a language other than English at home are entering today's schools should be exciting for us as educators—especially those of us interested in literacy. Bilingualism is an asset. The ability to communicate in two or more languages offers distinct advantages (Mackey, 1957). Understanding more than one culture is one of bilingualism's life-enhancing traits skill. Bilingualism affords many individuals cognitive attributes that support learning (Padilla, 2006; Cummins, 2005; Malakoff & Hakuta, 1991; Crawford & Krashen, 2007).

Unfortunately, bilingualism as a valued life skill and provider of positive cognitive attributes is rarely the focus when discussing the education of students who speak a language other than English at home. In fact, the term *bilingual* itself is illusory in public education. Children who enter our schools speaking languages other than English are given labels that too frequently diminish their linguistic gifts (see Table 3). These talented "bilingual learners" become English Language Learners (ELLs), English Learners (ELs), and Limited English Proficient (LEP). There is no mention of students' heritage languages or their bilingual abilities. Instead, they are viewed only in terms of their need for services; they are English as a Second Language (ESL) students or English Language Development (ELD) students. Such labeling is emblematic of a deficit approach to educating diverse learners. As soon as students' English deficiencies identify them as challenged learners, their assets become invisible.

Focusing on students' deficits is not simply a case of seeing the proverbial half-empty glass. The consequences of such an approach are far-reaching and cumulative. Students and teachers alike suffer as a result of such a focus (and its ensuing labels), and the outcomes are striking. Are teachers focusing too much on struggling students' weaknesses rather than on their strengths? Yes, according to Yvette Jackson, chief executive officer of the National Urban Alliance for Effective Education. In a presentation on reversing underachievement in urban schools, she argued that teachers must focus on students' strengths because their "focus is reality." Jackson said that educators are wrong to assume that "underachievers have no strengths." What's more, she warned against using labels such as *minority* and *disadvantaged* to support these assumptions. According to Jackson, "In order to close the achievement gap, educators shouldn't look at the lack of potential, but rather should have a fearless belief that all students have potential and teach according to that mind-set" (Jackson, 2008).

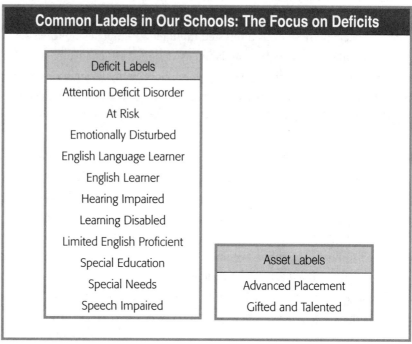

Common Labels in Our Schools: The Focus on Deficits

Deficit Labels
Attention Deficit Disorder
At Risk
Emotionally Disturbed
English Language Learner
English Learner
Hearing Impaired
Learning Disabled
Limited English Proficient
Special Education
Special Needs
Speech Impaired

Asset Labels
Advanced Placement
Gifted and Talented

Table 3

Labels can easily undermine the self-worth of a young student—especially one who may be new to the United States and working hard to learn English. Language is a key aspect of identity (Anzaldúa, 1987; Nieto, 2002; Portes & Rumbaut, 2001; Suarez-Orozco & Suarez-Orozco, 2001), and adolescence is a critical time for students' identity development. Students' linguistic attributes and abilities are closely scrutinized in junior high and high school. Carrying the ELL label can have damaging effects on an adolescent's belief in himself simply because his "limited" English skills are how he thinks others define him. Research shows that adolescent identity formation is significantly impacted by youngsters' perceptions of how others view them (Martinez, 1998; Wu, 2001; Tatum, 2003; Lewis, 2003). Being tagged as ELLs identifies students by the very attribute that most challenges (and often intimidates) them. Adolescents become increasingly self-conscious of their linguistic "differences" in secondary school, and for those who struggle with English, the ELL label exacerbates feelings of inadequacy.

Closing the Achievement Gap

The Effects of the Deficit Approach

Such labels and the attitudes that underlie them often have long-lasting effects on student engagement in school. ELLs are often alienated in school for a number of reasons (Olsen, 1997; Valdés, 2001). Within the larger issues of tracking and institutionalized racism, ELL education often leads to the formation of ELL "ghettos" (Valdés, 2001), where students who speak a language other than English make up the bottom track of their school. Students in such ghettos rarely interact with students in other tracks, furthering their isolation—socially, linguistically, and educationally. Students are aware of their placement in these ghettos, and although they may come to feel comfortable with some of their peers and teachers, they are not given the best opportunities to learn English or to excel academically. Many, over time, come to feel alienated and disrespected (Nieto, 2002; Cohen & Lotan, 2004). Additionally, students recognize that the ELL label inherently fails to acknowledge their heritage language. When students are told that the classroom is an "English Only" environment, they hear that their heritage language is not important, and does not matter.

When students' cultural backgrounds are not accepted and respected, their academic self-efficacy suffers, and their desire to learn dwindles. A language barrier is just one example of an obstacle that can, if not handled with care, create stigmatization and significant hardship for students. The bottom line is that many types of students struggle with reading in school. Students may have trouble reading because they are learning English, because they come from a home environment that does not place a value on literacy, or perhaps because they have been failed by the school system and passed along through the elementary years without significant, sensitive intervention. In all of these cases, students suffer at school because they feel as though they are defined by their weaknesses (and unfortunately, they are often right).

One of the outcomes of such feelings of inadequacy is low achievement. As students get older, those who struggle with reading are at an inherent disadvantage when it comes to keeping up with the demands on language and academic content. These students are often tracked with similarly situated students (Olsen, 1997; Valdés, 2001), and thus are never given a chance to receive the immersion in English necessary to best learn the language (Krashen, 1982; Padilla, 2006). And, students who feel stigmatized by their language, culture, race, or ethnicity are less likely to perform well on high-stakes assessments (Bandura, 1997; Steele, 2004). These negative effects on academic achievement are both rooted in and transcend issues of language. Students need to learn English in our public schools, yet they need to feel competent as learners in order to do so. The deficit approach that contaminates the education of these so-called English Language Learners and other struggling readers precludes students from doing so. This must be changed.

Breathing Fresh Air—Assets in the Classroom

Fortunately, changes can happen in the place where it matters most—the classroom. Despite the political contentiousness surrounding issues of bilingual education (Crawford, 1999; Kubota, 2005), the misguided attention given to high-stakes testing under No Child Left Behind, and the perennial underfunding of schools, it is classroom teachers like you who can most impact students by believing in their abilities to learn and succeed. Teachers are the ones who must approach the cultural diversity of today's students with one word in mind—*asset*—and often language is the tool with which authentic learning about diversity is built. Language offers a portal into another world, where students can see and share their different experiences and views. But in order for students to take full advantage of the opportunities that language presents, they must be encouraged to do so, and this encouragement starts with the help of a teacher who honors and respects the unique talents and attributes each student brings to the classroom.

Moll, Amanti, Neff, & Gonzalez (1992), refer to these unique talents as *funds of knowledge*, describing them as "historically and culturally developed bodies of knowledge and skills essential for household or individual functioning and well-being" (p. 133). Sharing these funds is what makes meeting new people fun and it also inspires us to travel the world and learn about cultures different from our own. Mining these funds of knowledge can help make diverse classroom settings both vital and rich. The funds transcend language, and they are at the heart of the asset approach to student diversity. Benson, Leffert, Scales, & Blythe (1998), in discussing the assets that communities can help youth build, make an important distinction between internal assets (motivation, self-efficacy) and external assets (a good school, high socioeconomic status). It is no surprise that recognizing student assets promotes academic success. While this may seem obvious, oftentimes it is necessary to make young people aware of the assets they possess and can build on at school. Enter the teacher; her positive regard of her students is essential.

Hypocritically, we require secondary students to complete courses in a "foreign language," yet we rush ELLs through sheltered English classes so they can join the mainstream as quickly as possible. Little or no attention is paid to students' heritage language (oftentimes, even if that language is both "foreign" and "required" according to the school) (Cummins, 2005). Meanwhile, schools struggle to hire bilingual personnel (administrators, teachers, aides, secretaries, support staff, and so on) to communicate with parents and the surrounding community. This is problematic. We are squandering our most precious resource—our students.

Ensuring success for non-native English speakers may seem like a daunting task, but the good news is that many of the strategies we use with native English speakers who struggle with reading will also work with non-native English speakers.

Valdés (2003) writes about the talents of the bilingual "young interpreters" she works with, urging us to reconsider what it means to be gifted and talented. Borrero (2006, 2008) takes this vision into schools and documents the impact of bilingual learners who gain status at their school site because of their bilingualism. Additionally, we find a burgeoning literature on language brokering, and the belief that translating and interpreting experiences may accelerate student development (Morales & Hanson, 2005; Tse, 1996; Weisskirch, 2005). Findings suggest that bilingual students have a lot to offer if given opportunities to succeed.

From Dependent to Independent Readers

As stated earlier in this chapter, a classroom full of students from many different cultural backgrounds is a classroom with a wealth of experiences and skills. The challenge, of course, is harnessing these assets, helping students become fluent readers in English, and closing the achievement gap. Ensuring success for non-native

English speakers may seem like a daunting task, but the good news is that many of the strategies we use with native English speakers who struggle with reading will also work with non-native English speakers. Research in reading reveals several skills that independent readers possess (Beers, 2003; Tovani, 2004).

Table 4 shows some of the skills that are necessary for independent reading, the difficulties students may experience with the skill, and ways in which teachers can assist students in becoming more independent readers.

The information in Table 4 poses several challenges for teachers who want to teach their students to become independent readers. Teachers often think that ELLs have vastly different needs from their native English-speaking counterparts. While that is true to some extent, the challenges listed in Table 4 apply to all students in many ways.

Most students benefit from thoughtful, strategic reading instruction—and this is especially true for our learners who struggle. For example, teachers need to spend considerable time building background knowledge and defining a clear purpose for reading. Native English speakers presented with a text about a culture foreign to their life experience might also have trouble understanding the text without a prereading exercise to build their background knowledge. Furthermore, as teachers who are experts in our subject area, we sometimes forget that not all of our students share our zeal for the content we teach. This fact makes it critical to clearly define a purpose for students before they begin to read. Another great challenge teachers face is helping students learn content vocabulary. Vocabulary deficiencies will hinder readers regardless of their native language. Focusing on these three important prereading tasks is key:

1. Activating or building background knowledge

2. Defining a purpose for reading

3. Supporting vocabulary development

Together, all three tasks will help students become successful independent readers.

We recognize that students who are learning English do pose unique challenges for teachers in the mainstream classroom. After all, if we didn't believe that, we

Helping Your Striving Readers Become Independent Readers		
Independent Readers . . .	Young readers need support because . . .	Teachers can help by . . .
use background knowledge to make connections between new and known information.	the reading may take place within a cultural context unknown to the student.	using texts from a variety of cultures and providing activities that help all students build background knowledge.
ask questions when they read in order to clarify and extend meaning.	the purpose of reading may not be clearly defined; therefore, the reader doesn't know what to ask. challenging vocabulary may result in frustration.	defining purposes for reading by providing a tool that will help students guide their own reading. providing multiple opportunities for students to identify and learn new vocabulary before reading.
make inferences from the text (read between the lines).	they may not have the background knowledge necessary to fully understand the text.	providing opportunities for students to build background knowledge before reading. giving students opportunities to talk about the reading with other students in order to make connections from the text to their lives.
separate the important from the unimportant to find the main idea.	the purpose of reading may not be clearly defined; therefore, the reader doesn't know what to ask. vocabulary may be too challenging, which causes frustration.	providing students with a reading guide with questions that will prompt them to re-enter the text to find the main ideas. providing multiple opportunities for students to identify and learn new vocabulary before reading.
use "fix-up" strategies to help comprehension when they get confused.	they don't always know when they are confused. they lack a repertoire of strategies to use when reading.	modeling thinking aloud for students. allowing students to work in pairs using a think-aloud protocol. teaching several comprehension strategies throughout the year with multiple rehearsal opportunities.

Table 4

wouldn't have written this book. But we believe that meeting students halfway and capitalizing on their strengths will produce independent readers. This is the approach we need to take with all students regardless of the label they may bear. Table 5 displays some important strengths that ELLs bring to the classroom and how these strengths relate to the skills necessary for independent reading.

An asset approach and the upcoming reading strategies

Focusing on your students' assets is not a simple task. All students bring different strengths and challenges into your classroom each day. It is difficult to remain focused on what your students can do when all of the standardized test score data show you what your students can't do and highlight how far "below grade level" your students are. We are not asking you to dismiss these data, and we are not saying that your students should not be reading at a level appropriate for their age; however, we are asking you to look beyond standardized test score data to reveal the strengths that your students possess. This may require you to utilize a range of assessments in your classroom, and give students multiple opportunities to show their talents. This takes time on your part and not all assessments may work equally well for all students. But we contend that the time you invest in helping your students feel comfortable sharing their stories, questions, ideas, and talents is time that will deliver rewarding dividends throughout the school year.

Helping your students become successful, independent readers is a process. If you begin this process together, with your students' strengths in mind, you can encourage them to see reading as more than just an academic skill that they must "master." You can help them see reading as a lifelong pursuit that can be difficult for everyone—even you—at times. This vision of reading and this relationship with your students that an asset approach embodies are vital to the presentation of the strategies in this book. We acknowledge that you have likely used some of the strategies that are presented in the upcoming chapters. We urge you to keep this asset approach in mind as you read about these different strategies and see if the combination—the approach and the strategies themselves—can help you find success with your striving readers.

Strengths of English Language Learners That Support Their Development as Independent Readers	
Independent Reading Skill	English Language Learner Strength
Using background knowledge to make connections between new and known information	All students have personal experiences that will help them relate to a variety of texts; the diversity of these experiences is often what makes reading (and learning) fun.
Framing questions in order to clarify meaning	If given a clear purpose, all students become more aware of when to ask questions in order to clarify or extend meaning. It is an unfortunate reality that ELLs are constantly questioning their English abilities; learning to ask "clarifying questions" is empowering.
Making inferences	Students routinely infer when discussing movies, television, sports, and so on with their friends. ELLs often utilize this skill as a part of acculturation—they "read" their new surroundings.
Separating the important from the unimportant	If given a clear purpose, all students can be more aware of which details are part of the "big picture" and which are not. ELLs often excel in this skill as a result of their experiences with translation and interpreting.
Using "fix-up" strategies (i.e. prediction, retelling, rereading)	English is a difficult language to learn. Students who are learning English have mastered strategies like retelling a story and rereading text.
Visualizing what they are reading	Regardless of language, most people have a visual representation in their head of what they are reading. As they learn more vocabulary in their target language (English), this picture will increasingly appear in English rather than the student's native language.

Table 5

Chapter 2

ONE SIZE DOES NOT FIT ALL:

Built-In Differentiated Instruction

dif·fer·en·ti·ate (dif-uh-ren-shee-eyt): –verb (used with object)

❖ to form or mark differently from other such things; distinguish

❖ to change; alter

❖ to perceive the difference in or between

❖ to make different by modification

We begin this chapter with a definition of the word *differentiate* because we believe that differentiated instruction is key to ensuring that all students are learning. Admittedly, this is a hot topic in educational research right now, but we think good teachers have been differentiating instruction since long before it was in vogue. So why has this topic suddenly gained so much traction among school

Using notes from the interactive read-aloud, students work in groups to discuss the text.

administrators and teacher educators? Take a look at the diversity in classrooms across the country and you will quickly see why this topic has come to the forefront of our field. While it used to be true that most ELLs were concentrated in California, Texas, and Florida (as we note in our introduction), immigrant enrollment is now on the rise across the country (Gándara, 2008; Goldenberg, 2008). Furthermore, the culture in which kids are growing up now is far different from the way it was a generation ago. Kids today are more media savvy, and thanks to cable television and the Internet, they have much more exposure to information than kids did even ten years ago.

As teachers we have to help our students see the relevance of our curriculum. Teachers of K–12 students are not alone in this challenge. We are constantly reworking our curricula to help our students understand the new challenges that public school teachers face. Many teachers argue that students need to learn certain material, whether or not they are naturally interested in the topic at hand. We don't necessarily disagree, but we do believe that differentiation has the potential to give students a deeper understanding of any given topic. As Tomlinson (2001) says, differentiated instruction is about "shaking up what goes on in the classroom so that students have multiple options for taking in information, making sense of ideas, and expressing what they learn" (1). Indeed, if teachers do "shake things up" as Tomlinson suggests, we believe students would gain more from their school experiences. While it is sometimes difficult for teachers to let go of the way we have been doing things for years and allowing students to demonstrate their understanding of content objectives in creative ways, we believe this is the only way we are going to close the achievement gap. For example, we know many teachers who have been assigning traditional research papers for years. However, with the advent of new technologies, why not allow students to research a topic and present their findings in the form of a video or podcast? We submit that students would work harder on the assignment because they would actually care about the work instead of just fulfilling the basic requirements as designed by the teacher.

Jackson (2001) argues that students who are labeled as low-performing students really need what she defines as the "pedagogy of confidence." She writes, "the pedagogy of confidence is based on the fearless expectation that all students will learn. When teachers practice this pedagogy, they do not doubt the potential of their culturally different students, and they switch their instructional focus from what has to be taught to how to maximize learning" (4). While believing in your students is important, it is only one element of differentiation.

As Jackson (2001) points out, taking into account the culture of your students is also a key to differentiation. Although some see the word *culture* to have complexities that teachers can't always deal with, if we substitute the phrase *life experiences* for the term *culture*, we may find that teachers are more able to take new approaches towards teaching students from many different backgrounds. By taking the emphasis off ethnicity, we are not denying its importance, but we do believe that stressing the experience is more fruitful when it comes to differentiated reading instruction.

We live and work in San Francisco, California, one of the most beautiful, culturally diverse, and expensive cities in the United States. Students in the San Francisco Unified School District come from very diverse backgrounds. We hear stories from our typically middle class teacher education students about their field work experiences in some of the city's high poverty schools. Here our teachers often experience a culture clash (Freeman & Freeman, 1994) as they work with students living in poverty. Think about all of the life experiences that converge in the classroom each day. While San Francisco is a relatively small city (in terms of area), each neighborhood has a distinct character. A student who lives in one of the rougher neighborhoods may have a hard time identifying with a teacher who hails from a more upscale area. And adding to the challenge, San Francisco students often attend school outside of their own neighborhood. If looked at from an asset approach, this blending of cultures creates learning opportunities for both teachers and students.

We believe that teachers across the country can provide such opportunities by acknowledging, respecting, and promoting the value of students' diverse backgrounds in class. As stated in Chapter 1, the first step for teachers is envisioning student's differences as inherent assets for learning in heterogeneous classrooms. Once teachers focus on student strengths, differentiation becomes crucial, because when teachers believe that all students can (and will) learn, teachers can see each students' (and their own) opportunities to teach each other and learn from each other. This vision for a cooperative, symbiotic learning environment is at the heart of differentiation. You still need to tackle the practical work of differentiating particular lessons, but you have set the foundation for it to unfold.

The View from a Classroom

Mr. Arnold, a history teacher in a large urban high school, has a class of 33 students in front of him. Of these 33 students, 12 are ELLs and 3 have been identified as special-education students with reading disabilities. The rest of the students are considered to have average or above-average reading comprehension.

Today, Mr. Arnold is teaching about war. He is trying to get his students to understand the concept of cause and effect, but he notices that six of the students are clearly not grasping the concept. Of the six students who are having difficulty, one is a Special Education student and the other five are ELLs.

Mr. Arnold tries to explain the concept in different words, but he is still explaining the concept in the context of a war. He sees that many of the students in the room are becoming listless. In order to address this situation, he decides that he will work with the small group of students who are having trouble and let the larger group of students move on to the next phase of the lesson.

Working with small groups is not a new practice for Mr. Arnold, as he has been teaching mixed-ability classes for some time now. At first, he was concerned that students might feel stigmatized if they were called into a small group in front of their peers, so over time, he devised a system in which he works with small groups on something every day. While most of the time the groups are focused on remediation, sometimes the groups participate in enrichment activities. In addition to students who need extra help, he also includes students in the group who have a clear understanding of the material. These students, he has learned, are a true asset to his teaching, because they can often explain things in ways that their peers can understand.

Mr. Arnold makes the following announcement: "Okay class, I need to work with the following students today in the front of the classroom: Omar, Jesse, Maria, Evan, Rene, Jennifer, Marcos, and John. If I did not call your

(continued)

name, you need to proceed with the instructions on the board." After Mr. Arnold makes sure everyone understands, the students go to the appropriate places in the room.

Mr. Arnold decided when he planned the lesson that he would use an article from the sports section of the newspaper that deals with a cause and effect relationship to scaffold the learning of those students who had difficulty grasping the concept. The article details the trading of a popular basketball player to another team and gives a variety of reasons for the trade. He tells the group he wants to use the newspaper article to further explore the topic of cause and effect relationships, and he wants the group to participate by completing a guided reading activity. Mr. Arnold allows the group to choose how they want to begin reading. The majority of the students want to take turns reading aloud, and Jennifer volunteers to begin. Before beginning the reading, Mr. Arnold suggests that the students pay particular attention to the reasons why the basketball player was traded. He asks them how they would like to take notes. Marcos suggests that highlighting would be a good way for him to keep track of things, while Rene says that listing reasons would be easiest for her. As a group, they all agree that they will either use a highlighter or take notes in the margins of the story.

The students share the reading responsibility, and after they have finished the article, Mr. Arnold has them compare their notes with a neighbor. After a few minutes, Mr. Arnold asks them to share with the larger group. The class seems to have grasped the concept. With this understanding, the teacher then has the students in the small group talk in pairs about cause and effect relationships in the context of war. Once he is satisfied that everyone understands, Mr. Arnold has the small group return to the large group and begin the next phase of the lesson.

A Critical Perspective of the Classroom

The interaction described between Mr. Arnold and his students is a complex series of events that captures the essence of differentiation. The term "differentiated instruction" has become what veteran teachers sometimes refer to as the "latest and greatest fad" thrust upon them by principals and central office administrators. Part of the reason, of course, is due to the increasing pressures school systems feel under No Child Left Behind and state education laws. While it is true that the term *differentiation* may be new to many teachers, it's almost certainly been part of formal schooling from the beginning. Think back to how schools must have operated in the days of the one-room schoolhouse! Those teachers certainly had to be masters at differentiating instruction not just for one grade but for up to twelve at a time! Let's take a close look at how and why Mr. Arnold chooses to do certain things during his lesson:

First, and most important, take a look again at the environment in which he works. He has a large class with students of varying ability, both academic and linguistic. Mr. Arnold's classroom probably looks a lot like one or more classes that you teach (or will teach) every day.

Because he has such a wide range of skills and abilities, it is important for Mr. Arnold to *set specific goals* for every lesson. In this case, he is trying to teach the concept of cause and effect. Notice that he is dealing with the concept in the context of his content area, social studies, but he is *not* caught up in the details of the particular war. This is an important point, because Mr. Arnold knows that if students can grasp the underlying concept of cause and effect, he can more easily teach them the details of the war at a later time. Moreover, his students are going to understand for the rest of the school year that historical events are often triggered by cause and effect relationships, so, when they read a textbook chapter, they will look for these relationships.

Mr. Arnold also does a great job of *monitoring his classroom for understanding*. He quickly recognizes that students are beginning to tune him out, and he changes his teaching strategy. Instead of letting the classroom deteriorate into a chaotic and unproductive environment, he reconfigures the groups. This scenario was only a possibility for Mr. Arnold because he had planned scaffolding activities ahead of time by anticipating where students might have problems. Additionally, he clearly spent a good deal of time planning the lesson in several stages so that he had an assignment ready for students who were not encountering difficulties with the lesson. By allowing his students who were ready to move on to do so, he limits their boredom and their temptation to get into "trouble." Thus, planning is a crucial aspect of differentiation. As a teacher, you must plan to provide multiple entry points for your students to access content. Yes, your lessons are strong, and designed to engage all students, but be sure to cast your net widely, providing learning opportunities that address all needs.

In this language arts classroom, a student annotates her book while the teacher reads aloud.

Moving from *whole class to small group instruction* is also a key element of Mr. Arnold's attempt at differentiating instruction. You'll remember from the example that Mr. Arnold often works with small groups of students, and includes students who clearly understand the material. You are probably wondering why he would risk boring these students if they get it and are ready to move on, but in fact, this is a smart thing for Mr. Arnold to do because he is not singling out the "struggling" students and he is giving their peers the opportunity to become leaders in the classroom.

Even more important, Mr. Arnold realizes that kids sometimes learn better from each other than they do from a teacher. Remember, Mr. Arnold tries to explain the concept in more than one way, without much success. He thinks that the students who are participating in the group can help him teach the concept in terms that their peers will understand. Moreover, by working with small groups on a regular basis, the chances are pretty good that *every* student will eventually get to be a peer teacher. There are about 180 days in the school year, and certainly there will be at least one day for each of his 33 students to shine.

Clearly, when they are in the small group, Mr. Arnold is trying to capitalize on students' outside-of-school interests. He chooses an article from the newspaper about a popular basketball player from their hometown team. While all the students may not be completely interested in this topic, as not everyone is a sports fan, they probably have at least a working knowledge of the subject matter. Furthermore, a newspaper article is written in a style that differs from a content-area textbook, a style that may help engage some students.

Throughout the class's small group time, student choice clearly plays an important role in Mr. Arnold's teaching. He empowers his students, letting them decide how to read the article (silently vs. aloud) and how to take notes on the article. Of course, it isn't blind empowerment. He structures their reading by suggesting what they look for ahead of time and he allows the majority to rule regarding note-taking strategy and manner of reading. You may feel the need to dictate more of those decisions at first, and that is fine, particularly when you are just starting to employ this style of teaching.

When we consider how we structure our courses, we have found that gradually releasing decision-making authority about projects and other assignments to students throughout the semester works well. However, it is important for us to teach our students to be independent learners. Students can only learn independence when they receive opportunities to make instructional decisions for themselves (no matter how small or inconsequential these decisions may seem to the teacher). Think about your own experiences in the workforce. Haven't you felt more empowered when you were given some authority to make decisions about how to tackle an assignment? This authority probably gave you a sense of ownership, which then, in turn, heightened your engagement. The same thing happens with students.

Differentiation and Acknowledging Teacher Assets

As a classroom teacher, your job reaches far beyond delivering content knowledge to thirty students between 8:00 A.M. and 3:00 P.M. every day. Teaching is far more complex than simply possessing content knowledge and imparting it to students. Do keep in mind your own skills and assets as a practitioner when considering the role of differentiated instruction and its impact on teaching.

Let us again look at the example of Mr. Arnold. This time we will investigate the assets he brings to the classroom as a teacher.

Confidence in Students

Mr. Arnold has confidence in students. This is clear in many ways from the lesson itself, but it is also evident in the way his classroom is set up. He believes that every student in his class can meet the objectives he has set, and he believes that the students themselves have abilities to help each other meet such objectives. As stated above, he has students working cooperatively, he allows them to do their work at their own pace, and he encourages them to find different ways to grasp the concepts of the lesson. This approach signals confidence in students because it suggests that Mr. Arnold is only one source of knowledge in the classroom. He sets the objectives for the lesson, but he enables his students to find their own entry points into the concept of cause and effect and its application. This belief in students' abilities—central to Mr. Arnold's practice—is a critical aspect of bringing an asset approach into the classroom. The belief that students are capable is a point of view we think most new teachers espouse. Sometimes student confidence is rattled, but typically it endures. The fact that you are reading this chapter and taking the time to reflect on your teaching suggests that you view yourself as a professional learner dedicated to becoming a successful educator. Your confidence in your students is an essential quality that frames and shapes your teaching.

Knowledge of Students

Getting to know your students is perhaps the single greatest responsibility of your job as a teacher. We trust that you entered the teaching profession because you love kids. Their eccentricities, naiveté, brilliance, and brutal honesty make the vicissitudes of teaching unparalleled by any other profession. Of course, we know you don't always like all of your students, but we acknowledge that you have dedicated your professional life to them and know that, to you, school is all about the kids. Alongside this reality is the fact that you get to know a lot about your students over the course of a semester or school year.

The beginning of the year, before we really know our students—and they know us—is a crucial time. We need to do all that we can to make accurate, valid, worthwhile assessments about our students during the opening days and weeks of school. The table on page 39 suggests some "getting to know you" ideas we can implement quickly and efficiently.

As the year goes on, you are continually assessing your students. From the moment you get your class list to the day you grade the final exam, you are building knowledge of your students. Of course, your assessments take on many different forms and serve many different purposes, but you are constantly developing a sense of your students and their development—as learners and as young adults. So, not only does Mr. Arnold know that some of his students are not grasping the concept of cause and effect because of their listlessness, but he is also able to draw on a wealth of knowledge about his students that he has developed over the course of the term. Yes, he knows which students are classified as ELLs by the school, and he knows which students have Individualized Education Plans, but his knowledge goes far beyond this. He knows what each student's current grade in his class is, what each student needs to do to improve it, and how likely they are to do so. He knows who is interested in history and why, and he knows which of his students have family members who are currently involved in the military.

Beyond all of this knowledge (and much, much more) about his students' academic abilities and backgrounds, Mr. Arnold knows that Jesse is a huge Kobe Bryant fan, and that Jennifer is a point guard on the school's junior varsity basketball team. He had Maria's sister in class two years ago, so he knows their mother, Esther, quite well. She serves on the PTA and is entirely dedicated to her daughters' education even though she, herself, never graduated from high school. Additionally, Mr. Arnold knows that two of his students are having trouble in their current English class and are in jeopardy of being removed from the course—a step that would make graduation a near impossibility. Mr. Arnold knows that Evan, who came in a few minutes late with a Taco Bell bag sticking out of his backpack, likely skipped math class again today. The smell of fresh cigarette smoke wafting from Evan's jean jacket makes Mr. Arnold wonder what else Evan has been smoking, and how much he will be able to focus on the reading.

Begin the Year Building Community:
Things You Can Do

Ask students to share something about themselves for their first assignment.
Example: Have students make a poster that tracks their own personal cultural history.

❖ Encourage students to think about their uniqueness.

❖ Provide a model from previous year students or share your own personal cultural history poster.

❖ Give your students ample time to complete the poster; allow them to finish at home as needed.

Provide opportunities for students to get to know each other in class.
Example: On the first day of class, create a form where students answer questions about themselves and then try to find classmates with the same answers.

❖ Help students learn and use one another's names quickly.

❖ Use ice-breakers to get students used to working with each other.

❖ Join your students in ice-breakers to show that you, too, are part of the classroom community.

Create the classroom environment together.
Example: Invite students to contribute posters, art work, writing samples, articles, and similar items to put on the walls.

❖ Encourage students to take pride and ownership of the classroom.

❖ Show pride in your students' work.

❖ Create a rotating bulletin board with updates of students' work and interests (inside and outside of your classroom).

Content Knowledge

Content knowledge is something that grows over time and may require a lot of work during the evenings and weekends, but as a teacher you possess content knowledge and you need it. If you do not have appropriate content knowledge the first time you teach something, you surely realize it and know exactly what you need to learn. Again, using Mr. Arnold as our example, it is important to note that he has strong content knowledge in history—particularly American history and World War I. His belief in his own content knowledge in this area enables him to teach his students a larger concept, cause and effect, via studying the onset of WWI. He also has knowledge of current events. He usually sticks to major news stories and developments in the war in Iraq, but today he read about a major trade made by the city's professional basketball team. He is not a huge sports fan, but he knows enough about the business of sports to see the connection with his lesson. Again, this is just a slice of Mr. Arnold's content knowledge, but it is key to his ability to differentiate his lesson. Content knowledge will be a major asset for you, too.

Combining Teacher and Student Assets

In Chapter 1 we pointed out the necessity of acknowledging students' assets in today's diverse classrooms. This perspective is especially essential for teachers of ELLs. Not only do students possess linguistic assets as burgeoning bilinguals, but their languages most often point to larger, broader cultural identities and backgrounds. As adolescents, most middle and high school students are in the midst of developing their own identities. We all know that middle and high school students are tremendously self-conscious and very concerned with the perceptions of others (especially peers), so students' cultural backgrounds often clash with the dominant school culture. Especially for middle schoolers, a classic reaction to such tension is to try as hard as possible to fit in. Being unique in middle school is typically something kids prefer to avoid.

As a teacher, you can probably empathize with your students who, on some level, are searching for a sense of themselves at school. You also know that the social aspects of secondary school are powerful and potentially ruthless. Thus, it is important to find some place for your students to feel comfortable and confident at school.

Students who have a sense of self-efficacy with some part of their academic lives are far more likely to be engaged in school and to overcome the inherent challenges that adolescence, and secondary school, entail. Oftentimes, this sense of self-efficacy comes from opportunities outside of the classroom. Student athletes or members of the school band, for example, often feel a sense of belonging and accomplishment through school-related—or school sponsored—activities. This is important because even though such beliefs may not be bred in the classroom, they keep students in school, and they foster a sense of belonging to the school community.

Academics can also provide a source for student self-efficacy. Most Advanced Placement (AP) students take pride in that label and embrace an academic identity through their accelerated proficiency in some content areas. Likewise, a young writer may love his English class, for example, and his participation and development make up a part of his sense of identity as a student.

AP students are often members of the debate team, participants in student government, captains of their respective sports teams, and enrollees in several other AP courses and exams. For a multitude of reasons, few of these students are ELLs. It does not take long to realize that many teenagers who have not achieved a comfort level at school may not identify with their student status, and tend to avoid all school activities— academic, athletic, and extracurricular.

Despite these truths, research tells us that immigrant students are perhaps more eager to learn than their nonimmigrant classmates (Portes & Rumbaut, 2001). Additionally, unlike the perspective held by many Caucasian students that "trying in school is not cool," most immigrant students prioritize effort as the key factor in their success. Thus, for many students who struggle academically the desire is there, but the opportunities for success may not be. We believe that the combination of the belief in both student and teacher assets is an essential foundation for effective differentiated instruction. Such instruction is a way to provide opportunities for successful learning for all of your students—ELLs, reluctant readers, students with special needs, and fluent English speakers alike. Such opportunities can make all the difference for students who have experienced nothing but failure, deficit labels, and exclusion at school.

Chapter 3

WE'RE ALL IN THIS TOGETHER:

Tap Cooperative Learning to Foster Students Strengths

The importance of incorporating cooperative learning into classroom practice for all middle and high school students, and especially for those who are ELLs and striving readers, is substantial. In fact, many of the strategies discussed in chapters 4–7 elucidate the role that cooperative learning can play in developing strong readers. When working with proficient and developing readers, cooperative learning is especially necessary because reading is a social act. Sure, we read on our own, and we can comprehend text independently, but we truly engage with the content

Students working cooperatively.

of what we read when we talk to others about our thoughts, questions, findings, and connections. Some struggling readers and, in particular, ELLs, are often denied this social aspect of reading because they are frequently labeled as deficient readers and isolated (Olsen, 1997; Valdés, 2001). This isolation can come from the school (by way of practices like pull-out ESL and rigid teacher expectations) or the student (through feelings of inadequacy).

Cooperative Learning and Reading

In the snapshot of the classroom that follows, Ms. Godinez models effective strategies to promote cooperative learning. Specifically, she is using a version of reciprocal teaching (Palinscar & Brown, 1984) in her junior-level chemistry class in a large, urban high school in California. As you will begin to see from the student responses, the class comprises heterogeneous learners. Not only do they possess different knowledge of and experiences with science, but they also have different reading abilities. Ms. Godinez is using small group activities that tap the various assets her students have as young chemists and as developing readers to promote effective reading strategies for all of her students.

Ms. Godinez: At the end of class yesterday we spent some time in our new groups. Is everyone sitting with your new group?

(*Some students nod, others blurt out a reluctant "yes," and others get up to move to new tables. While they do this, Ms. Godinez puts up an overhead transparency that lists students' names in groups of four. As students get settled, they comment and ask questions.*)

Manny: Why we changing groups?

Donna: Yeah. I like my old group. Why we keep changing?

Ms. Godinez: Good questions. We are going to change groups a lot this year. You guys have a lot to teach each other. In fact, today we are going to start a new activity in our groups that we are going to use when we read from our book in class.

(continued)

(*Ms. Godinez writes the words* reciprocal teaching *on the board and points to them.*)

Ms. Godinez: Okay, we are going to call this group activity *reciprocal teaching*. Who can tell me what the word *reciprocal* means?

Lucy: It means, like, to give back.

Ms. Godinez: Thanks, Lucy. Perfect. As a verb, *reciprocate* means to give back, so as an adjective, *reciprocal* means equivalent or mutual—the same. What do you think reciprocal teaching in your groups is going to be about?

Juan: Teaching each other.

Diane: Giving back to each other?

Ms. Godinez: Yes, kind of. Just as you normally do in groups, you guys are going to be working together to teach each other different parts of what you are working on. Today we are going to start reading chapter 3 in the book, and we are going to use reciprocal teaching to make sure we all understand what we are reading.

Ben: What if we don't need help understanding what we read?

Ms. Godinez: That's a fair question, Ben. Reciprocal teaching gives you the opportunity to help others in your group by showing them how you go about reading a section of the book. Likewise, you can see what your group members do when they read and perhaps learn something from them.

Ben: So we are going to teach each other how to read?

Ms. Godinez: Kind of, but not exactly. Here's how reciprocal teaching works. On days when you come in and see *Reciprocal Teaching* written on the agenda, you will have four index

(continued)

cards on the front of your lab table. (*Ms. Godinez passes out the stacks of cards to each table.*)

Ms. Godinez: As you can see, written on each card are the words *predictor*, *clarifier*, *questioner*, and *summarizer*. We are going to—

Jasmine: (*interrupting*) We did this already . . . in Ms. Jones's class.

Ms. Godinez: Great, Jasmine. You will be able to help us then. What are we going to do with these cards?

Jasmine: You have to look at the pictures and stuff and then tell everyone what you think the chapter will be about. It's easy.

Ms. Godinez: All right, good. You are getting a little bit ahead of us, though. What do we actually do with the cards?

Brian: You pick one, and then you do that job.

Ms. Godinez: All right, exactly. In your groups you will be picking a card each day for reciprocal teaching. This card will determine your role, or your "job" as Brian says, for that day's activity. Before you choose your cards for today, let's spend some time talking about each of these roles. Jasmine got us started on the predictor role already. Tell us again, Jasmine, what does the predictor do?

Jasmine: Easy. You make predictions.

Ms. Godinez: Yes, but what do you actually do in the group? What does the role entail?

Jasmine: Ms. Jones told us to look at the pictures and stuff like that and tell the group what we think would happen next.

(continued)

Ms. Godinez: That's a good start. We are going to do things a little bit differently in here, then. Yes, we are going to use the pictures and graphs and tables in the book, but during reciprocal teaching we are actually all going to read the same section of the book to ourselves, and as we do so, each of us will be thinking of our role. So, like Jasmine says, the predictor today will be reading pages 60 to 64 with everyone else, and her job will be to present her predictions to the class based on what she has read. A key part of her role, and everyone's role, is to answer the question *why*. So, as the predictor, she needs to think about what the rest of the chapter is going to be about, but she needs to be very specific about *why* she thinks this will happen. This idea of answering *why* is crucial, because not only will each of you be helping each other understand the chapter, you will also be sharing your reading strategies with your group.

(Ms. Godinez and the class go on to discuss the details of each of the different roles before students initiate their reciprocal teaching.)

Cooperative Learning for Culturally Diverse Students

As the example from Ms. Godinez's class begins to show, when used effectively, cooperative learning allows for students to learn with one another. In this environment, this means that students will get to learn about their peers' wide-ranging linguistic and cultural experiences. In linguistically diverse classrooms, this may mean learning about classmates' heritage languages or comparing specific structures of English with analogous structures in different languages (Rickford & Rickford, 2000). In this way, students learn about each other, learn from each other, and learn about themselves. Language is the vehicle through which this learning takes place, but it can also be a portal into a much more complex and potentially fascinating discovery of life's diverse experiences. When teachers establish environments that promote reciprocal learning for their students, significant power emerges from the fact that the teacher is not in direct control of group work. It is empowering for students to realize that their teacher is not the only one in the classroom with important knowledge and experiences to share. And this realization is at the heart of an asset approach to literacy instruction—not only for struggling students, but for all students.

Affective Aspects of Cooperative Learning

Cooperative learning sends a number of important messages from teachers to students:

- ❖ First, you show your students that you trust them enough to have them learn together.

- ❖ Second, you recognize the knowledge and abilities that all your students have.

- ❖ Third, you offer students a safe space (or perhaps even a community) that gives them a sense of belonging.

This last point is particularly important for ELLs, and even more important for the development of ELLs' literacy skills. As previously stated, the deleterious effects of the ELL label often result in feelings of isolation and inadequacy. These feelings plague students and can often define much of their school experience. In fact, Freeman and Freeman (2007) remind us that nervousness, boredom, and anxiety can all deter student learning. Allowing students to work in groups eases emotional duress and helps all students access learning.

Feelings of isolation clash with the mind-set students need to become successful readers. At school, students need to feel that they are a part of something larger than themselves, and inside the classroom, groups may help give them that feeling. Groups do not have to be permanent, nor does group work have to dominate instruction. Students may want to fulfill a given role or secure a good grade.

For those students who are resigned to their isolation from the class or school community, group work creates a low-stakes opportunity for inclusion. In addition, students may be willing to take more risks in small groups because the teacher may not be present.

Perhaps more significant for struggling students is the fact that small groups offer opportunities to learn directly from peers, and students benefit immeasurably when they realize that they are not alone in their academic (or reading) challenges. It can be empowering for a student to see peers struggle with and learn material that he or she already knows. Similar worth is gained from learning with the help of another student in the group. In this sense, ELLs are unique because they can harness their linguistic aptitude in a language other than English. Two ELLs (even two with different abilities in a shared heritage language) may find comfort and confidence in sharing their own experiences with a given text. Group work can enhance these feelings of comfort and confidence for even the most dejected ELLs.

Cognitive Aspects of Cooperative Learning

The effectiveness of students using a heritage language (L1) to help other students learn English (L2), makes the most compelling case for cooperative learning in linguistically diverse classrooms. The potential of this kind of cooperative learning is heightened when it comes to reading because reading is about comprehension, and in groups, students are great at helping one another grapple with meaning. In a discussion group comprised of members from similar language backgrounds, ELLs can use their L1 to talk about aspects of the text. Such group discussion can reveal the challenges ELLs face as readers, but perhaps more important, the discussion can also reveal the different strategies ELLs employ as readers. Providing students with the opportunity to talk about reading in their heritage languages can be fruitful for ELLs because they can use their L1 skills to do so. Students rarely get this opportunity in the classroom, but it is a crucial facet of cooperative learning for two reasons: First, it enables students to transfer their linguistic skills from L1 to L2 (Butler & Hakuta, 2004; Padilla, 2006), and second, it utilizes an asset that bilingual learners possess—making meaning in context. Regardless of students' academic backgrounds in their L1, they are constantly employing meaning-making strategies to understand one another. Group work can give students a chance to teach each other these strategies and apply them to reading.

You do not need to (and often cannot) follow every detail of your students' L1 discussion—especially if they are speaking a language that you do not understand. Your trust in the power of their bilingual discussion enables them to take group learning seriously, and to use their bilingualism as a tool with which to help each other. Clearly, this approach to group work takes time to set up and organize; however, the dividends are significant, as students feel linguistically liberated and enjoy "showing off" their prowess as bilinguals. This feeling is likely a new one for many ELLs in the classroom, but it is essential for them to realize their own assets when it comes to language and making meaning in social settings.

ELLs respond well to the opportunities that group work presents when they are able to explore and express their linguistic abilities in their heritage languages. When using their native languages, students are still learning the strategies you are teaching (summarizing, making generalizations, predicting, and so forth) but it is easier for them to practice these skills in their native languages. The process of transfer (students using their L1 skills and applying them to L2) is fostered through effective cooperative learning, and students can rapidly apply their L1 meaning-making strategies to their literacy development in L2. Of course, at some point, all students in the classroom need to use English as their primary language, but inviting students to use their native languages helps them build confidence in their ability to complete the same tasks as their English-speaking peers. Consider your students' L1 as a scaffold to help support their academic growth.

In addition to providing opportunities for linguistic transfer, group work is essential for the way that ELLs think about reading and processing text. As discussed, the affective benefits of group membership and a sense of belonging are helpful to ELLs. Additionally, the social nature of groups helps students who are learning English to process meaning more effectively and efficiently. Talking about texts and reading is a meaning-making process, and whether students are taking on different roles within the group or explaining their interpretations of a given passage, the ability to listen to and talk about reading is significant. ELLs may be more willing to take risks and express their interpretations of a text in a small group away from the watchful eyes of the teacher or the whole class. Or, if attempting to fulfill an important role within a small group, an ELL will be more likely to ask a fellow student for help. These authentic opportunities for self-expression and conversation around texts and reading are exactly what ELLs need in order to develop their academic English. Rarely do students have such opportunities in whole group activities. ELLs may grow accustomed to the isolation of their label and shy away from taking the in-class risks necessary for learning (especially when it comes to reading).

Students need to hear and use academic English on many levels. Cognitively, ELLs need to acquire new lexical items when developing academic English, so the comprehensibility of the input (Krashen, 1982) they receive when learning new terms is pivotal. The lexical items themselves may be brand new, so you must double your efforts to provide the contextual information that will enable ELLs to understand the meaning and function of these new academic terms. Repetition, visual representations, graphic organizers, and cognates are all useful tools for promoting comprehensible input, but even more basic is the language used in the classroom during a given lesson. You supply academic language when you introduce a given lesson or unit, but all students (and especially ELLs) benefit from hearing academic language in context from their peers. As a matter of fact, this should be the goal when teaching academic language—providing opportunities for students to use it in authentic contexts.

Effective group work greatly enhances the comprehensible input required for you to meet this goal with ELLs. Students hear the terms and concepts in different ways from different individuals, in different settings. Thus, small groups provide the opportunities for ELLs to hear their peers use (and perhaps even explain) academic English at a level or in a manner that is more closely aligned with their linguistic skills. Peer-to-peer conversation around the term *osmosis*, for example, in a science class (complete with such conversational features as *likes* and *umms*) may really help an ELL grasp the concept. Inviting students to use their L1 can also aid comprehensible input, but as students strive to learn academic language, conversations in English are key. Cooperative learning creates opportunities for such conversations.

Cooperative Learning as Differentiation

Together with the other strategies in this book, teaching that provides opportunities for cooperative learning is simply good pedagogy. Yes, it is central for effectively promoting the assets of all students in your classroom and enhancing their literacy skills, but the positive effects of having students work collaboratively in class extend far beyond reading and linguistic development. In many ways, collaborative learning can automatically differentiate instruction for students because it takes the focus away from the teacher as the "provider of knowledge" and places students at the center of their own learning. Different students from different backgrounds with varying abilities are invited to learn together. Students may not always see the value in this, nor will objectives always be met for all of the group members, but the process of trying to work together is an inherently worthwhile endeavor—for students and teachers.

Effectively planning, creating, and implementing group work is an exceptionally challenging job, but the benefits are immeasurable. In essence, your greatest asset as a teacher—your knowledge of your students—is put to the test when you try to figure out how they can best work together and teach each other without your direct help. This task is both daunting and tremendously empowering, but it really gets at the heart of what teaching is all about—helping students learn and become lifelong learners. Differentiated instruction can work only with this goal in mind. We want all students to engage in content at their own level and have the opportunity to explore it as far as their interests carry them—perhaps even beyond what *we* know. Groups provide students with a glimpse of extended learning by allowing them to learn with and from each other.

This sociocultural approach to learning is central to effective literacy instruction—especially when it comes to drawing from and uncovering the assets that your students bring to the classroom as readers. Their experiences are valuable, their backgrounds are important, and their bilingualism is useful. Cooperative learning enables them to display these attributes and use them to learn.

Think-Pair-Share

Reciprocal teaching is a great strategy for helping students digest complex content, but it may be a strategy that you work towards, as teachers don't always feel comfortable giving up so much control, especially with classes that have widely varying ability levels. Using a strategy called Think-Pair-Share (Lyman, 1981) may be an easier place to start for some teachers.

Another advantage of using Think-Pair-Share is that you can determine starting and stopping places for students and can therefore differentiate for groups that are less advanced. For example, when working with a group that has many striving readers in it, you may ask them to stop reading and to pair-up-and-share more often than a group that has many higher ability readers.

The Strategy at a Glance

Think: Students are given a question before they begin reading. They are told to think about the question as they read. This step highlights the importance of setting a purpose for reading. The students then read the text. It is important to chunk the text into manageable parts for the students. In science class, for example, where there are many complex concepts presented in relatively few pages, the text needs to be divided by the teacher, particularly for ELL students. You may have the students take a few moments after reading to write a response to the question or to just think about a response that they will share with their partner.

Pair: Students are told to work with a neighbor. There are any number of ways to accomplish pairing. In some cases, you may want to let students work with a friend—especially the first time you try this strategy, as it will build confidence. As students feel comfortable using the strategy, you may pair them in different ways.

Share: This is the most important part of the strategy. Depending on how you set it up at the beginning with your students, they will either share what they have written with their partner or they will verbally share their thoughts. At this point you should be circulating around the room listening to student responses.

Why Think-Pair-Share?

This strategy gives you a lot of bang for your buck. You can see that it is a relatively easy strategy to use, and students don't need lots of detailed instructions in order to execute the strategy. It is fairly straightforward: give the students a question or questions, have them read, pair them up, and have them talk about their answers.

While this may seem like a simple strategy, when teachers use it, the information they can learn about their students is incredible.

If the text is chunked into manageable parts, you can tell where kids are having problems with comprehension. This seems particularly important in content areas such as science that are so dependent upon vocabulary. When you are talking to pairs of students, you can instantly know and fix where they are getting confused, instead of not knowing where the trouble spots are until the quiz or exam comes along. Furthermore, working with students in pairs instead of the entire class makes it possible for you to get to know your students' needs on a more personal level. Knowing this information will allow you to make strategic grouping decisions and enable you to spend time with kids you think are struggling.

From a student perspective, this strategy is great because students get to talk to one of their peers and check their answers in a nonthreatening environment. As discussed previously in the chapter, our students will succeed at learning to the extent that they feel comfortable, supported, and part of the classroom experience. While this strategy allows for peer interaction, it is *structured* interaction, so you can control your students' tendencies to get off-task. Many teachers hold their students accountable by grading the process of their work, meaning students may not have to have the correct answer, but they do have to demonstrate their best effort.

In the End . . . Group Work Works

Both strategies discussed in this chapter focus on the positive relationship between literacy and interaction. We all know that learning thrives with student-to-student interaction. ELL students, in particular, need this interaction so that they can improve their English skills while also learning the content necessary for mastery of their coursework. There are probably thousands of group work strategies out there, but these are two that have been around for a while and both enable students to make sense of the content. It is easy for us to forget that students are not experts in our content area and that not all of them are as interested in our content area as we are. For some who are striving to read at grade level, having a peer to work with will make a difference.

Group work has gotten a bad rap among more experienced teachers in the past few years. We argue that group work that is well managed can be an effective instructional practice.

Comprehension has three important aspects: the reader, the text, and the outside influences brought to the text. This is important for teachers to consider as they assign reading for content areas in which students are not yet proficient. Collaboration enables striving students, who may have limited "world experiences," to tap into their peers' value systems and ideas about the world beyond the classroom; which will in turn boost the striving students' ability to comprehend new material. Isn't this what we do every day with our friends? When we go to the movies and talk about it afterwards, aren't we all bringing our background experiences and our knowledge of the context of the movie to our interpretation? You can see why it makes such good sense to support collaboration in our classrooms.

Tips

Tips for Your Classroom:
Students Learning With Each Other

Reciprocal Teaching

❖ Decide on roles that you find most effective (e.g., clarifier, questioner, summarizer, predictor, vocabulary master, coordinator, visualizer, and note-taker).

❖ Approach the setup and explanation with thoughtful deliberation.

❖ Model a sample group with volunteers prior to starting.

❖ Chunk text appropriately.

❖ Check in frequently with groups.

Think-Pair-Share

❖ Prepare students for the strategy by walking them through the steps before providing the text.

❖ Encourage students to work with different partners.

❖ Chunk text appropriately.

❖ Pose questions that provide multiple entry points for students with different reading abilities.

Part 2

Essential Reading Strategies

Kids who read with proficiency are empowered with essential skills they'll need to survive the demands of contemporary life. And kids who don't read are at risk. It's that simple.

—Alan Sitomer, *Teaching Teens and Reaping the Results*

Chapter 4

GETTING STUDENTS READY TO READ:

Preview Texts and Scaffold Vocabulary

Prereading activities are critical if we want our students to construct a deep understanding of a text. As Wilhelm, Baker, & Dube (2001) remind us, nearly all the student confusion about a text stems from the fact that we did not do a good job at the beginning of the lesson in accessing background knowledge that our students likely already have! For content area teachers, prereading is perhaps even more important. Think about science and the specialized vocabulary that students must understand before they embark on reading a text. Without this basic knowledge, there is likely to be a great deal of misunderstanding from the beginning.

For struggling readers, the significance of prereading activities is magnified. Students' background knowledge is defined by their life experiences. All students bring something unique to what they read, including students who are learning English, students who arrive with different academic and cultural backgrounds, or those who have difficulty processing text. As proficient readers, and especially as teachers, we often overlook the fact that the texts we use in school (especially textbooks) are highly codified cultural artifacts. In American public schools, this means that texts often reflect the dominant English monolingual mind-set of the

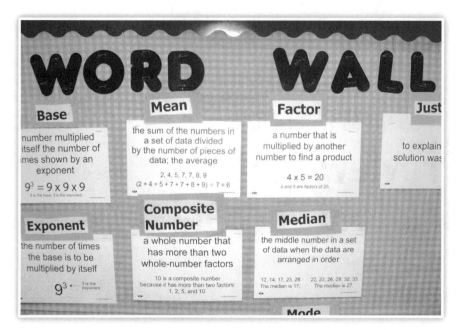

Word walls, appropriate for all content-area classes, are an effective way to remind students of key vocabulary words.

country and our academic institutions. Therefore, not only do we need to address the academic language and key vocabulary terms required for comprehension prior to reading, but we need to make the text itself approachable.

Utilizing Student Diversity Around Text

Given the fact that students' life experiences impact the prior knowledge that they bring to a given text, the diversity of experience is expanded in heterogeneous classrooms. In such classrooms students not only come from many different cultural and academic backgrounds, but the fact that some students speak languages other than English at home means that the way these students approach language, communication, and text may be different than their native–English speaking classmates. For example, in our experiences with Latino adolescents in California, oral communication is the most important use for language (English and Spanish) outside of school. Written communication and reading may receive less attention, as students are often the bilingual interpreters or language brokers (Tse, 1995) for their parents. This definitely affects the background knowledge that these students bring to texts in school.

In the Classroom

Use your first assignment to build a sense of classroom community. For one of your first homework assignments of the year, have students bring in a "cultural artifact" that is important in their lives. Start class by having students free-write about why this item is important to them, and what the importance of the item might show about them. Do this along with your students and set aside time for everyone to share. Make the activity low-stakes and informal, but use it to send a message to your students: who they are is important in your classroom.

Again, it is key that teachers regard their students' diverse backgrounds as assets in a classroom of heterogeneous learners. It is especially important for teachers to hold this view when it comes to ELLs and other striving readers whose experiences may be largely ignored by a system that simply sees them as deficient readers. The students with whom we work bring exceptional knowledge from their experiences as bilingual interpreters to the texts they encounter in school. Yes, these students need to spend more time, perhaps, with the structure and vocabulary of a given text, but the problem-solving and comprehension strategies that they bring to any form of communication—including their own complex conversations with peers about a wide array of topics—are highly advanced.

Utilize your young interpreters. At the start of the school year, recruit your bilingual students to help you translate a letter home to parents that is written in their native language. The letter might outline your expectations and goals for the school year, or it can be an invitation to visit your classroom or attend back-to-school night. This letter will show parents that you not only care about their language and want them to participate in their child's work in your class, but it will also show your students that you value their language, culture, and home life.

Again, when teachers recognize, promote, and draw on their students' differences, their students thrive. Diversity becomes an advantage—a strength—in the classroom. To this end, prereading activities are essential. Prereading not only involves teaching students the strategies essential to engaging with texts, but it also entails finding out where students are in relation to a text, what they bring to the text via their own interests and backgrounds, and what they will need to successfully engage with a given text. Thus, prereading is an opportunity for open-ended questioning and informal assessment. As teachers, we must meet our students where they are, and to do this we must find out where they are as we begin a text.

The **View** from a Classroom

Making the Text Accessible by Previewing

On a recent visit to a middle school in Northern California, we observed third-year teacher Mr. Moore's sixth-grade humanities class in an inner-city public school, where 80% of the student population speaks a language other than English at home and 85% of students qualify for free or reduced lunch. The transcript below comes from the beginning of the lesson Mr. Moore used on the morning of the second day of school.

Mr. Moore: Before we start reading Chapter 1 today, we are going to spend some time looking at the details of this book together. So, I want you to leave all of your materials, except for your humanities notebooks, at your desks, and bring your chairs and notebooks up to the front of the room.

(continued)

(*Students arrange themselves in the front of the first row of desks—directly in front of the whiteboard. Mr. Moore has posted color copies of the textbook pages on the whiteboard.*)

Mr. Moore: In front of you is Chapter 1 of the textbook—

Jaime: (*interrupting*) You cut up the book?

Mr. Moore: Actually, Jaime, I made color copies of the pages, but they are exactly the same as the pages of your books.

Alma: Is that the whole chapter? It looks so short.

Mr. Moore: Good question. You tell me. Is this the whole chapter?

Mitch: No way—it's too short.

Leslie: It is, because I see the questions on the last page.

Mr. Moore: Excellent, Leslie. How else would we know it was the whole chapter just from looking at it?

Leslie: Well, in our books we could turn the page to see if Chapter 2 was next.

Mr. Moore: Okay, good answer. How else would we know this is the whole chapter?

Randy: I can see the last part before the questions is called the summary. That means it is the end.

Mr. Moore: Excellent, Randy. What do you mean when you say "the last part?" How can you tell that there are different parts of the chapter?

Randy: Because it says it.

Mr. Moore: What do you mean? Where does it say it?

(*Randy gets up and points to a section of the text.*)

(continued)

Mr. Moore: Okay, but why is this a "part" of the chapter?

Miguel: It is in big letters and has a space above it.

Mr. Moore: Great! What do we call those big letters?

Susanna: Bold?

Jackie: Fonts?

Mr. Moore: Okay, good. You are actually both right. We can see that the "summary" is a section of the chapter because the letters of the word itself are different from the other letters. Let me ask you this. What is the title of the chapter?

Carla: Introducing World History.

Mr. Moore: Great. How do you know it is the title?

Carla: Because it is on the first page.

Jackie: It is in big letters.

Juan: It is on top of the picture.

Mr. Moore: Okay, this is great. Many of you are noticing very important details of this chapter already. What I would like each of you to do is take out your journals and take three minutes to write down all of the different details that you notice about this chapter in front of you. We have already mentioned "book parts" like the title, the pictures, the different parts, and the questions at the end. These are all great. I want to keep looking at this chapter and write down all of the other things you notice that appear on these pages.

Any questions?

Roberto: Yeah. I don't get it.

(continued)

Mr. Moore: Okay, no problem, Roberto. Let's help him out. What type of things might you write down on your list?

Leslie: I know. How about the map on page 2?

Mr. Moore: Excellent. What else?

Juan: I don't know what you call it, but those words, right there (*pointing to a word on the first page*). The ones that are kind of sideways. They look different.

Anna: Italics.

Mr. Moore: Excellent. Does everyone see the word Juan is pointing to? Do you see how the letters are slanted, or as Juan said, "sideways"?

These words are called "italics." Let's everyone write that down.

(*Mr. Moore writes the word on the board.*)

Does this make sense to everyone? Remember, there are no right or wrong answers to this. I just want you to think about all the different features in this chapter and write them down.

(*Mr. Moore walks around students' chairs as they work on their lists, answering questions and offering praise for good items. After three minutes, he asks students to share their lists with a partner.*)

Mr. Moore: Okay, great job with your lists. Now, I want you to start thinking about these different items on your list, and why they are a part of this chapter. Who wants to share one of the items from your list?

Ricky: Bold words are darker because they are more important.

Mr. Moore: Okay, Ricky. Good start. Come up here and show us all a bold word.

(continued)

(Ricky points to the first bold word in the chapter—"culture" on page 3.)

Mr. Moore: Great. Ricky is exactly correct. These words that are darker are called "bold" or "boldface" words. What do you mean, Ricky, when you say they are "more important?"

Ricky: They stand out. They are different from the others. We are supposed to remember them, I think.

Mr. Moore: Great. Let's everyone look at the boldface word, *culture*, on page 3. What else do you notice? Why is it important?

Nicky: Just like the other bold ones, it tells what it is right after it.

Mr. Moore: Okay. I think I am following you. Tell us more.

Nicky: It is like a dictionary, kind of. It says what the word means right after the bold. Like for *culture* it says, "a shared system of values and beliefs." It defines it.

Mr. Moore: Excellent. So, the boldface words in our textbook this year are our key vocabulary words. Whenever you browse a chapter (like we are doing now), you will see the important words in bold. These are the words that will go in your vocabulary notebook.

(This discussion continues as students share all of the different features they noticed: pictures, graphs, maps, captions, headings, subheadings, summaries, italics, drawings, and so on. Students also share that they notice there is no page that features only written text—that is, there is some text element or graphic that breaks up the written text on every page. Mr. Moore encourages the students to do as much of the talking as possible and towards the end of the discussion talks about book publishing, and the fact that publishers put these features in the text to help us all better understand the material.)

Using Text Preview

It is crucial that Mr. Moore take the time he does to introduce his students to the humanities textbook they will be using for the school year. Not only is he introducing his students to this specific text, but he is also teaching them (or perhaps reviewing with them) vital prereading strategies. We refer to this prereading strategy as *text preview*. As the name implies, text preview is nothing revolutionary. Teachers have been working with students to preview texts for years. However, although not novel, text preview cannot be overlooked— especially in secondary classrooms. As a matter of fact, text preview is even more important in middle and high school as students encounter more varied and difficult texts.

> *Text preview is not necessarily tied to content, and for that reason, you can use it with a science textbook, a math textbook, or even a Shakespearean tragedy.*

The objective of text preview is simple. Young readers need to learn how to use all of the features of a given text to help them comprehend it. Good readers do this instinctively. Somewhere along the line, we, as teachers, learned to do it as well. However, young readers are rarely taught how to do this effectively. As Mr. Moore demonstrates, with a sixth-grade humanities textbook, text preview takes time. Only the beginning of his lesson is described, but it is clear that there are numerous text features that he and students will be discussing:

- ❖ Chapter headings, subheadings
- ❖ Book parts such as table of contents, introduction, bibliography, index, and so on
- ❖ Illustrations, graphs, charts, maps, and other graphics
- ❖ Captions
- ❖ Fonts—bold, italicized, oversized
- ❖ Summary/Review questions

Quick Tip: Text preview in action

In addition to the directions at the end of this chapter on how to set up text preview in your classroom, we believe there are some essential factors to keep in mind when planning for a text preview:

1. Use text preview early in the year, and revisit it often.
2. Provide a visual representation of the text for the whole class to look at together.
3. Allow students to be the experts about the features of the text—have them teach each other.
4. Talk to your students about the publishing process and why texts are designed the way they are.

Text preview is essential for obvious reasons. Most important, this strategy teaches students how to use all of the possible resources available to them to make meaning of text. Text preview is a way to show students that texts are about words and making meaning of sentences, paragraphs, and pages. Additionally, authors, editors, and publishers offer other features to help readers comprehend content. This is an important message for all students, but it is especially important for struggling readers because it has the potential to tap into an asset that many students develop before they learn technical vocabulary: the use of context clues. ELLs, for example, may in fact have a lot to offer during text preview, as they are accustomed to the process of trying to make meaning from text they may not entirely understand. Text preview is a way of sharing different methods for using context clues to encourage students to make the most of the texts they encounter.

Mr. Moore is just beginning the text preview process in the example in the box on pages 60–64. The time that he puts in now, at the beginning of the school year, will pay dividends as the weeks and months go by because he will continually build on the foundation that he and his students have established around the key features of this textbook. The approach that you take to teaching text preview is up to you, so make it your own and have fun with it. We suggest that you start by asking students what they normally do when they get a new book—a textbook, a novel, a picture book, a manual, and so forth. They are likely to name the strategy of *browsing*, which is definitely a worthy starting point.

Mr. Moore will continue his text preview, facilitating conversation with his students about the different features of the text they notice. He will continue to ask them questions such as "Why is this feature included?" and "How will you use this feature to help you when you read?" At some point, he will segue from a discussion of the general features of the text to a discussion of the actual content of the material (in this case, Chapter 1 of the textbook). It is important that he make this shift explicit for students, so they can start to see that the features they just discussed as a part of the text preview are now going to be applied to the content of the chapter.

This shift to the content of the text marks an important distinction in this discussion of prereading strategies. Text preview is not necessarily tied to content, and for that reason, you can use it with a science textbook, a math textbook, or even a Shakespearean tragedy. The point is to make explicit the previewing skills that good readers use to comprehend text. Text preview is best used, then, to set up other prereading strategies such as making predictions based on different sections of the text, or using a Think-Pair-Share (Lyman, 1981, McTighe & Lyman, 1988; Nessel & Graham, 2007) to begin to elicit students' prior knowledge of the content to be learned (see pages 52–53 in Chapter 3 for details about these strategies). For example, Mr. Moore may follow this section of the text preview by asking students to look at the picture and map on the first page of the chapter and *Think* for 30 seconds about why the book starts with these images, then form a *Pair* with another student, and *Share* their ideas with each other.

Scaffolding Vocabulary

One of the prereading strategies that Mr. Moore did teach after the text preview was vocabulary. He utilized the boldface print in the text and had students begin to engage with the key vocabulary terms of the chapter. The text preview enabled students to use the features of the text to deepen their understanding of key terms by taking the following steps to fill out a grid (for an example of a completed grid, see Figure 3):

1. Copy the sentence from the text in which the word appears.

2. Write the definition of the word as it appears in the text.

3. Write the definition in your own words.

4. Write the word in a sentence of your own that expresses the definition of the word.

5. Write a synonym.

6. Write an antonym.

7. Write the closest translation of this word in another language (optional).

8. Draw a picture of the word to show its definition.

Mr. Moore modeled this activity on the overhead projector with the whole class helping him out for the first word. For the second word he asked for volunteers to share their answers as he filled in the grid on the overhead projector. For words 3–8 he had students work in pairs as he circulated around the classroom monitoring

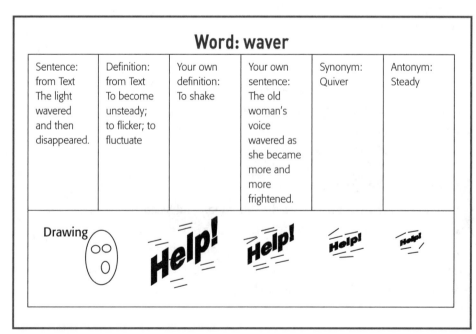

Figure 3: Example of a completed vocabulary grid

students' progress and answering questions. Students were directed to begin reading the chapter after they had finished their words. When everyone was finished, Mr. Moore went through the whole grid with the class, asking questions and clarifying any confusion about the words.

There are several features of Mr. Moore's vocabulary lesson that are important to note—especially when considering that over 80% of Mr. Moore's students are ELLs. Perhaps most important is the fact that vocabulary is being taught in context. This is a huge factor in literacy development and makes vocabulary a key prereading strategy. Students need to learn new words in relation to larger concepts.

In the Classroom

Find ways to remember words—together. As you introduce new vocabulary terms to students, help them think about surefire ways to remember the word. Model this practice early in the year by thinking out loud about the ways in which you remember new words. For example, you may say to them, "*Assuage* may sound like a tough word, but I have an easy way to remember it. It contains six of the same letters, in almost the same order, as massage—and both bring comfort and relief." After modeling, you can begin to ask students about their own successful ways of remembering words, and even list and post their collective strategies.

In secondary classrooms, this means that they need to learn words that they encounter in texts. This is especially significant for ELLs and struggling readers because lexicon is the single most challenging aspect of text. When students encounter a word that they don't know, they need to use other reading strategies to make meaning of a given chunk of text. As we know, most students are constantly making use of familiar strategies to work their way through a challenging text, but this takes time—and, as we all know, time is a key variable in reading—especially when reading in class or reading for a test. For struggling readers, an unknown word often begins a process in which they focus intently on the troubling word or chunk of text, begin to fall behind the "normal" pace of their classmates, panic, and become frustrated. Perhaps even more intimidating for students is the fear of reading out loud in class and, in front of their peers, encountering a word they don't know. This in turn leads to a feeling of failure and a sense of "I am no good at reading." A terrible outcome which far too many students experience.

To avoid this, we need to acknowledge that learning new words is challenging, and take the time to prepare students for words they are going to encounter in texts. In order to provide students with the time they need to think about a new word in different ways, they need multiple opportunities to comprehend it.

This approach to scaffolding vocabulary not only caters to students' different learning styles, but it shows students that vocabulary development is challenging and that learning new words takes time and effort—not just for struggling readers, but for everyone. In other words, vocabulary development is a lifelong process.

Tips for Your Classroom:
Getting Your Students Ready to Read

Text Preview

❖ Get two copies of your textbook or other reading material (make color copies or request copies from the publisher; you need two copies because pages are printed back-to-back and, otherwise, you won't be able to preview every page).

❖ Tape the chapter pages together so students can see the entire chapter at once. (Post pages on the whiteboard.)

❖ Use text preview for the first chapter of the year, and revisit it until students recognize all the attributes of the text.

❖ Use text preview as a way to teach academic language about texts (title, bold, italics, chapter, and so on).

❖ Use text preview to explain how books are constructed.

Vocabulary Grids

❖ Start early in the year and make vocabulary grids a part of your weekly routine.

❖ Teach vocabulary words in context—even better, use words that students will soon encounter in their reading.

❖ Encourage students to use their grids to practice new words (in their writing, and orally in class).

❖ Encourage students to keep all of their grids in one place so they can keep track of the words they are learning.

Chapter 5

WE LEARN TO READ BY READING:

Harness the Power of the Interactive Read-Aloud and Monitored Sustained Silent Reading

As Frank Smith (1986) wrote more than two decades ago, students become better readers by reading. For those of us who teach, this idea is certainly not earth-shattering, but for many policy makers, administrators, and others concerned with increasing student achievement, it's a simple idea that seems to have been lost. The ever-increasing number of non-native English speakers, and their struggle to learn academic English so that they can perform on state assessments, highlights the need for making the read-aloud and sustained silent reading programs routine in secondary school classrooms.

The pressure to increase student achievement seems ever more present in our schools today. No Child Left Behind mandates that every child will be a proficient reader by 2014 (www.ed.gov) —a tall order for many schools to meet. In response to the increased standardized testing in schools, teachers can participate in numerous programs designed to help them and administrators increase student achievement.

One way to engage students in silent reading is to provide them an area in the classroom that is more comfortable than the typical classroom desk.

Certainly not all of these programs are bad. Indeed, some of them are useful as they provide supplementary materials for a skilled teacher to use in the classroom. Unfortunately, however, it seems that some of these programs aim to replace the good judgment of a skilled teacher by providing scripted or "teacher-proof" instruction. What school administrators and program creators must realize is that there is no substitute for a great teacher! We have met many wonderful teachers who teach kids how to think, but we have yet to meet a program that is able to consider students' academic and social developmental needs, let alone craft scaffolds to help students who are struggling to grasp a concept.

As classroom teachers ourselves, we know you face myriad challenges when it comes to accelerating students' reading levels so that they can pass the required state exam. Struggling readers and students learning English, in particular, need qualified and skillful teachers who can expose them to language in a variety of ways. Our

> *You, and you alone, know your students best and know what will help them most.*

teaching and research experiences in public secondary schools in California and Texas have made it abundantly clear to us that you, as a classroom teacher, possess the greatest potential for giving *all* of your students the opportunity to succeed. This may seem obvious, but this is important for you to acknowledge, because there are many others who play a role in your students' lives, and there are many others who play a role in what you are expected to teach in your classroom. You, and you alone, know your students best and know what will help them most.

We know that you might be required to teach from department, school, or district reading programs. This does not mean that students cannot become successful independent readers, nor does it mean that you cannot employ effective teaching strategies to help them become strong readers. But it does mean that you will have to make some important decisions about the time that you do have with your students, your faith in the mandated program, and your confidence in your abilities if you plan to be civilly disobedient in teaching literacy. The practices highlighted in the passages that follow are aimed at making your decisions easier. The interactive read-aloud and monitored sustained silent reading are effective, powerful, and relatively easy practices that, as research demonstrates, produce success for readers of all different abilities.

The Interactive Read-Aloud

Perhaps one of the best ways of modeling good reading skills is by reading aloud to your students—and by *interactive* read-aloud we mean inviting rich questions and rich conversation as part of the read-aloud. Irene Fountas and Gay Su Pinnell (2006) define it this way:

"By *interactive read-aloud*, we mean that the teacher reads aloud to students, but both the teacher and the students think about, talk about, and respond to the text. Both the reader (in this case the teacher) and the listeners are *active*. The teacher is reading the words aloud, but in every other way, the students are processing the language, ideas, and meaning of the text. Occasionally, the teacher stops briefly to demonstrate text, talk, or invite interaction. These pauses are intentional and planned to invite students to join in the thinking and the talking about the text. There is no way to predict what students will say, of course, but that is part of the appeal of this interactive way of working with texts. The conversation is grounded in the shared text" (p. 216).

While reading aloud to students is a staple of the elementary classroom, as students get older, educators often assume that students are too old for the pleasures of the read-aloud. From our own experiences as middle and high school English teachers working with diverse populations, we know that all students, regardless of age, love to be read to. No one can resist the magic of a powerful read-aloud—and the learning benefits are immeasurable. Indeed, we argue that reading aloud is one of the best things you can do for your students. In *Reading Aloud and Beyond: Fostering the Intellectual Life With Older Readers* (2003), Frank Serafini and Cyndi Giorgis mince no words when they make the following statement about both the appeal and benefits of reading aloud to older students: "Reading aloud with students supports their development as readers and writers, fosters their love of reading, improves reading skills and abilities, encourages them to continue reading throughout their lives, and yes, even increases their achievement on standardized tests. . . . Reading aloud is just as important for older readers as it is for young ones and should occur every day, into the intermediate-grade classrooms and beyond" (p. 1).

The Benefits of the Interactive Read-Aloud for Struggling Readers

All students benefit from having a teacher read aloud to them, but perhaps the students who benefit the most are those who struggle with their reading. It seems obvious that a student trying to learn English, for example, would benefit from hearing the target language as much as possible. Anyone who has taken a foreign language knows that the curriculum includes both oral and listening skills. Moreover, an interactive teacher read-aloud can be a confidence builder for all students because, regardless of their native languages, all students bring some experience and knowledge of their language system. Freeman and Freeman (2007) remind us, "Whether students are reading in Spanish or Chinese, they

> *The interactive read-aloud is perfect for making learning transparent by walking students through the comprehension strategies you use.*

use their background knowledge and the same linguistic cueing systems and psychological strategies. All languages, despite their surface differences, use symbols to represent meanings" (p. 132). And you, as an expert reader, can display your command of the language system you are teaching students, providing them with powerful lessons about how their target language works and how proficient readers go about making sense of a written text. The interactive read-aloud is perfect for making learning transparent by walking students through the comprehension strategies you use.

While you can teach these meaning-making strategies in a variety of ways, the interactive read-aloud provides a uniquely potent and authentic context for students to process the information. One of the most powerful attributes of the read-aloud for struggling readers is the fact that you, the teacher, are generating the text orally and inviting them to respond with their own questions, thoughts, and connections. Just as you know your students, your students know you, and your relationship is an indispensible part of your students' literacy and linguistic development. For example, research on second language acquisition tells us that the first stage of comprehension depends on the comprehensibility of the input (Krashen, 1995; Padilla, 2006) the learner receives. Your students spend the beginning weeks and months of the school year building strategies to make the input that they receive from you (e.g., your voice, your body language, your movement around the room, your writing, your teaching strategies) comprehensible. They rely on you to provide multifaceted, meaningful input, just as you should rely on them to provide you with feedback when they cannot understand you. Thus, the interactive read-aloud is a supremely powerful tool for building this linguistic relationship. As you model effective reading strategies during a read-aloud, your students reap the linguistic benefits. Reading researchers and educators (Krashen, 1982, 2004; Laminack, 2009) agree that good readers do the following: predict, ask questions, make text-self-

Students in this classroom are given the first 15 minutes of each class period to read self-selected books.

world connections, visualize, use fix-up strategies, and make inferences. Reading aloud—and inviting rich conversation around the text—presents the perfect opportunity to model all of these strategies for your students.

Additionally, for students who might feel they are not smart if they don't pronounce every word correctly the first time, or understand every vocabulary word on the first reading, seeing and hearing a teacher *miscue*, which Goodman (1979) defines as departing unexpectedly from the text, can be a confidence-building experience. And it becomes your opportunity to explain that all readers *miscue* as they work with a text and attempt to construct meaning. As readers actively engage with a text, they may skip over words, substitute words, or in other ways depart from the text as they work toward meaning. Miscues that don't interfere with meaning are actually a sign of reading strength. That's because reading is not a precise process of "getting the words," it is about using all the cueing systems—semantic, syntactic, pragmatic, graphophonic—to interact with the author's text and to draw from one's own language, background knowledge, and view of the world to construct meaning. Further, every student in your classroom can benefit from a review of these skills when they face a difficult text.

Tips for Your Classroom:

Benefits of The Interactive Read-Aloud for All Students

❖ Being introduced to rich content and transcending the boundaries of experience.

❖ Expanding literary knowledge of different authors, genres, illustrators, and learning to evaluate the quality of each text.

❖ Absorbing comprehension-monitoring strategies.

❖ Receiving demonstrations of hr. expert oral reading and fluency.

❖ Understanding that it is okay to reread a difficult passage.

❖ Learning that it is okay to miscue as long as the miscue doesn't interfere with the meaning of the text.

❖ Discovering the role of punctuation in written language (e. g., quotations, periods, commas).

❖ Acquiring new words and expanding vocabulary; learning techniques for figuring out unknown words.

❖ Building relationships with specific books, authors, topics, and genres and developing a sense of themselves as readers.

❖ Bonding with classmates and teachers and sharing the uniquely intimate experience of getting lost in a book together.

❖ Being introduced to the intellectual benefits of interpreting and discussing texts.

❖ Learning to think hard about a text, ask questions, suggest connections, and in all ways, engage with a book, peers, and teachers.

In the Classroom

Start each class period by reading aloud a quote, a poem, or a short passage of prose to your students. Use this as a way to begin class, and have fun with it. Read things that you like—your favorite poet, a columnist in the local paper, a current event. You can even have "Friday Joke Day" where you read aloud a joke to your students. The goal of this activity is simple—provide all the benefits of the interactive read-aloud to your students by reading aloud to them every day. In the process of beginning this routine, you will not only be modeling good reading strategies, but you will be sharing personal details about yourself through what you read with your kids and creating an all-important bond with them. As the year progresses, encourage students to provide or read the passage for the day.

The View from a Classroom

Effective Interactive Read-Aloud

We visited an alternative high school in Northern California and witnessed a wonderful example of read-aloud. Ms. Meyette teaches in a school where students are sent for their "last chance" to graduate from high school. For many different reasons, her students have been asked to leave the other public schools in the district, and are now at a school

(continued)

where they take a humanities class, a science class, and a math class each morning and then go to work in the afternoons. The excerpt below comes from Ms. Meyette's humanities class. The group is mixed-age (ages 15–18) and definitely mixed-ability. Students come from many different cultural backgrounds, and most are students of color. In January, we observed Ms. Meyette use an interactive read-aloud to help students analyze Roethke's poem "My Papa's Waltz." The text of the poem, and a partial transcript of the lesson follow.

My Papa's Waltz

– Theodore Roethke

The whiskey on your breath
Could make a small boy dizzy;
But I hung on like death:
Such waltzing was not easy.

We romped until the pans
Slid from the kitchen shelf;
My mother's countenance
Could not unfrown itself.

The hand that held my wrist
Was battered on one knuckle;
At every step you missed
My right ear scraped a buckle.

You beat time on my head
With a palm caked hard by dirt,
Then waltzed me off to bed
Still clinging to your shirt.

(continued)

Ms. Meyette:	Okay class, today I am going to read a poem to you called "My Papa's Waltz." You all have a copy of the poem in front of you, right? Before I read, can anyone tell me what a waltz is?
Lara:	I think it is a fancy dance.
June:	Well, I think it is an old-timey dance.
Ms. Meyette:	Anyone else? Well, both of you are right. It is a dance that was popular many years ago. Your grandparents might know about the waltz. If I can get a volunteer, I will show you how to do it.

(*Several students volunteer.*)

Ms. Meyette:	Okay Eddie, come up here and we will demonstrate the dance.

(*Teacher and student do a quick waltz as other students watch and giggle.*)

Ms. Meyette:	Thanks, Eddie . . . you are a great dancer!
	Now, let's move on. I am going to read the poem out loud and I want you all to follow along or just listen to me. (*She reads the first stanza.*) So what is going on here?
Ana:	I think this guy is drunk!
Ms. Meyette:	What makes you say that?
Ana:	Duh, he has whiskey on his breath, and he is, like, stumbling around.
Ms. Meyette:	That is a good observation, Ana. Who agrees with Ana? (*Some students nod and raise their hands.*) Okay, are there

(continued)

other ideas? (*Silence . . . wait time.*) Okay. We will come back to that. Let's move on for now. (*Continues reading.*) Does anyone know what *countenance* means? (*Silence.*) No one? (*More silence.*) Okay. Can someone tell me a strategy we can use for finding out the meaning of *countenance*?

Javier:	Look it up in the dictionary.
Ms. Meyette:	Okay, good. That is a good strategy, Javier. Why don't you go ahead and look it up for us while we think about other ways to find its meaning. Who else has an idea? Without a dictionary—what is another strategy we can use?
David:	You can look at the rest of the poem. The stuff that comes next.
Ms. Meyette:	Good, David. Tell me more.
David:	Well, just look at the next line . . . It might mean sad, because the word *unfrown* is on the next line.
Ms. Meyette:	Okay, does anyone agree with David?

(*A few hands go up in agreement.*)

Mara:	That doesn't make sense to me. *Unfrown* does suggest that the mother was sad, or maybe mad, but countenance wouldn't also mean sad . . . that would be repetitive.
Ms. Meyette:	That's good. I think both of you are on to something. Are there other ideas? What would *countenance* mean in line 7?

(continued)

(*More wait time.*)

Brian: I think it just means something about her face.

Ms. Meyette: Why?

Brian: 'Cause her face couldn't unfrown itself. It is like she could not smile or something like that.

Javier: (*interrupting*) It means "appearance . . . the look or expression of the face."

Ms. Meyette: Great job—both of you. Brian, I like how you used the context clues in the poem to get the definition for countenance. So, if countenance means someone's facial expression, what do we know about the mom in the poem?

Jamie: She could just be, like, telling them to grow up. You know . . . she could just be irritated 'cause the dad is drunk and he is bouncing around the room with the little kid.

Ms. Meyette: That is a very good observation, Jamie. Why don't we make a note by that stanza and we will come back to it later.

(*Lesson continues.*)

Tips for Successful Interactive Read-Aloud

❖ Establish a read-aloud ritual, creating a predictable time and designated place for daily reading with clear expectations for students.

❖ Choose mostly high-quality literature including culturally relevant texts, but read aloud from a range of material demonstrating the ways in which different genres are crafted (letters to the editor, sports reports, memoirs, mystery thrillers, science fiction, and so forth).

❖ Introduce new authors, topics, and genres and invite students to weigh in on their favorites; keep track of the books and materials you share and note those the class likes best.

❖ Activate student background knowledge before reading; introduce new concepts and words that may be new to your students.

❖ Ask questions that invite students to make predictions about the content of the books, the author's intent for writing the book, how the book might connect to the students' lives or other books they know, and so on.

❖ Allow students time to talk with peers so they can process information; promote discussions before and after the read-aloud.

❖ Model the reading process by thinking aloud.

❖ Help your students develop a sense of themselves as readers with clearly defined reading preferences.

The lesson in this classroom continued for thirty minutes, as Ms. Meyette read the poem aloud to students and stopped to ask questions. By the end of the lesson, the students had more questions than they had answers. That is exactly what Ms. Meyette wanted to happen. The next day, she planned to take them further into an analysis of the poem, and because they had so many questions, the students would be forced to reenter the text in order to answer those questions. Ms. Meyette is not only helping her students become better readers, but she is also teaching them how to think critically. The students in this class are average-ability students. There is a good mix of native and non-native English speakers, but all of the students were engaged in the lesson.

Ms. Meyette encouraged engagement through her read-aloud and presentation of the poem. It certainly helped pique their interest when she demonstrated what a waltz was before reading the poem! We also see that Ms. Meyette was concerned that the vocabulary might prove to be a stumbling block for her students and, accordingly, helped them figure out the meaning of unknown words.

In the Classroom

Encourage your bilingual students to read aloud in both English and their native language in your classroom. You can do this by bringing in texts in students' home languages and having them read aloud and translate for the class. You can also post important quotes, classroom rules, and signs throughout the room that reflect the multiple languages of your students. Your goal is for students to embrace their bilingualism as an important asset in the classroom. Send this message to them by conveying your own interest in language and reading, and by encouraging them to share their bilingualism.

Beginning with the title and continuing through the second stanza, Ms. Meyette spent a good amount of time on vocabulary. She demonstrated a couple of different ways that readers can deal with vocabulary. With *waltz,* she just asked someone what the word meant and they knew. No need to belabor it any further. The word *countenance* posed more of a problem. Nobody in the class really knew what the word meant, although after using context clues, they were able to figure it out together.

Ms. Meyette could have easily told the students to read the poem and answer the questions that followed. Had she done so, some kids would have been able to perform successfully, but many would have been stymied from the beginning and would have given up in frustration. By reading the poem aloud, Ms. Meyette demonstrated multiple strategies, including different ways to acquire vocabulary, which is particularly important for struggling readers.

Tips

Tips for Choosing Successful Read-Aloud Books

❖ At first, choose books with fairly straightforward plots (the fewer characters and subplots, the better) as a way to help kids engage and follow while they learn to listen.

❖ Select from Young Adult (YA) novels (see our recommendations, p. 108); YA books are a hit because the characters are close in age to students and often face similar challenges.

❖ Look for books in the 200–250 page range; again, at least initially, smaller books are ideal because you can finish before students lose interest.

❖ Choose several books and allow your class to vote on the one they want after you book-talk the titles you have selected.

❖ Keep gender in mind; your female students will listen to and discuss books about sports, but typically boys do not enjoy teen romances.

In the Classroom

Read one of your favorite plays (short stories and novellas work as well) out loud with your kids over the course of several weeks. Use the play as a "filler" lesson for days when you finish early, encounter a change of schedule, or simply want to circle up with your students and read. Make it low-stakes and fun. Students can pick parts to read, or you can hand out badges with characters' names on them. Participate in the reading (perhaps as the narrator) and pause at different points to ask questions, make predictions, and clarify. Encourage everyone to read. It will become a routine the entire class comes to look forward to.

In sum, regardless of the content area, reading aloud to students comes with immense benefits. While language arts teachers may enjoy a wider range of reading material from which to choose (poems, prose, drama, science fiction, and so on.), all content areas require reading, and the more complex and specialized the vocabulary and content knowledge, the more support ELLs and challenged readers need. As Serafini and Giorgis (2003) remind us, "There is no substitute for reading aloud. No other experience or instructional strategy can capture the mood and enjoyment of a piece of literature. Reading aloud is about more than increasing standardized test scores and developing more capable decoders. It's about teaching students *why* to read, not just *how* to read. It's about inviting them into the world of literature and exposing them to the joys of reading and the fantastic story worlds available in books. It's about teaching them what pleasures await them between the covers of a good book" (p. 11).

Monitored Sustained Silent Reading

Free reading time, or sustained silent reading (SSR) is a rare occurrence in secondary schools these days. This is likely the result of the growing number of state standards, and the pressures to increase student achievement on tests. However, monitored SSR, when coupled with explicit reading instruction (Kamil, 2008), is a powerful way to increase students' reading comprehension and fluency, and most important, improve their attitudes towards reading (Pilgreen, 2000). And free reading also brings more good news: no tests! The primary purpose of providing kids with time to read each day is to give them a more positive outlook towards reading. The extra benefit of this activity is that it increases student achievement. In Krashen's (2004) meta-analysis of more than one hundred studies on free voluntary reading programs, both student attitude and student achievement improved in every study. Krashen's findings confirm, in many ways, our commonsense knowledge about readers. People who read are confident readers who enjoy reading and typically have stronger vocabularies. What's more, skillful readers tend to be more skillful writers, too; indeed, every time we read, we get a lesson on how to use written language to craft an engaging message (Smith, 1988). Therefore, it stands to reason that allowing students to read their own chosen texts for a designated period each day would strengthen their reading and writing ability (and ultimately help them perform better on standardized tests).

Students in this middle school classroom have a wide selection of choices for Monitored Sustained Silent Reading as well as a comfortable place to read.

Closing the Achievement Gap

Guidelines for Setting up a Monitored Sustained Silent Reading Program

❖ Establish a routine time for SSR (e.g., first 15 minutes of class).

❖ Allow students to read whatever they want (as long as it is school appropriate).

❖ Ban tests and quizzes connected to SSR.

❖ Monitor all aspects of SSR. Ideally you should develop your own tracking system and require your students to keep track of the books they read, the number of pages they read each day, the new topics, genres, and authors they explore, and so on. We recommend Atwell's *The Reading Zone* (2007).

❖ Encourage students to talk with each other about what they are reading (during a designated time—not during SSR).

❖ Take students to the library regularly if you don't have a classroom library.

❖ Allow students to give up on books that don't interest them.

❖ Participate in SSR and send students the message, *reading is important*.

Tips for Building and Maintaining an Irresistible Classroom Library

❖ Collect a wide variety of books from which students can choose and allow them to select their own reading material.

❖ Invite your community to donate books by holding a "Gently Used Book Drive."

❖ Organize your classroom library, with your students' help and input, so kids can easily find the books they are looking for.

❖ Include books on tape, which are especially helpful for striving readers and ELLs.

❖ Encourage your students to create a "Check This Out" bulletin board. On index cards they write a brief summary of a book they recommend to their peers and place it in a due date envelope. Students can regularly peruse the board when they are looking for a new book to read.

❖ Work to develop a classroom that "talks books," where students develop potent relationships with particular books, authors, genres, topics, and so forth, and routinely think about and discuss the books they are reading and want to read.

Note, however, that here, we are referring to *monitored SSR*. Michael Kamil (2008) makes it clear that SSR on its own may be of limited value, but states when it is coupled with explicit instruction from knowledgeable professional educators, it is effective in promoting reading growth. Kamil argues the following: "*teachers* and *instruction* are the critical variables in the relationship of recreational reading to reading ability . . . . We have to emphasize instruction if we want our students to achieve at optional levels . . . . The data we have collected suggest that reading practice needs to be coupled with reading instruction while maintaining the integrity of instructional time. [We need to focus on] the truly effective combination of reading practice, high-quality instruction, and knowledgeable teachers" (p. 40).

From our experience as teachers who have implemented SSR in our own classrooms, we feel the most important tip we can give you is to follow through with the program. If you don't stick to a regular schedule with clearly defined, consistent expectations, your students won't think SSR is important. To that end, we suggest you start small. If you know that you can't afford to give up 15 minutes every day of the week, then start with 15 minutes two or three days a week. Once your students get into the SSR routine, they will anticipate it each day and will be happy if you can add more time later in the school year.

SSR can be particularly effective if it is a schoolwide initiative. Many students think that reading is reserved only for their language arts class. They are often surprised to learn that their content-area teachers read for pleasure. Modeling this behavior for students is powerful, and it will improve student achievement. In fact, we would argue that if you do nothing else, implementing SSR will increase standardized test scores.

The Accountability Issue

We have talked with many teachers who love the idea of SSR but are concerned about student accountability. To guarantee successful implementation, your first order of business is to establish very clear expectations for your students; for example, SSR is about *silent* reading—not searching for a book or talking out loud with peers. Students need to understand that they are to begin every SSR period with a book in hand, which means they must conduct their book searching and selection *before* they come to class.

In the Classroom

Begin a voluntary book club for your students. As you get to know students' reading interests and abilities, encourage them to read with one another. A relatively easy way to do this is to open your classroom to students one day a week at lunch, and have them come in and meet as a book club. You can help them with their first few gatherings, but they will take it from there. You can also sponsor a book club as an after-school activity. Most often, students simply need the space to get together, and the encouragement of a teacher to recommend books and ideas for discussions. While you do not need to read all the books students are reading, the more you know about their particular interests and book choices, the more effective book club mentor you'll be.

Once you've established your rules, you will want to find easy-to-implement ways to monitor and keep track of the books your students are reading and the number of pages they read each day.

While it is important to remember that SSR time should be as stress free as possible for students, there are effective ways to ensure students are taking their reading time seriously. Research findings from Livaudais (1985) and Giles (2005) suggest that adolescents enjoy talking with their friends about the books they are reading. In Appendix A (page 136), you will find a reproducible handout that you can give your students in order to structure their talking time. However, we caution that this should be used only occasionally (e.g., once a grading period) so that students are not sent mixed messages about their independent reading time. The form encourages students to talk only briefly about the book—after SSR; it does not ask them to go into great detail. You might consider creating a space in your classroom in which to post the completed discussion forms and invite students who are looking for new reading selections to peruse the forms for advice from their peers about SSR reading favorites.

Closing the Achievement Gap

Middle school students slip their book recommendations into library book pockets to entice their peers into reading their favorite books.

The Benefits of SSR for Striving Readers

Challenged readers benefit immeasurably from SSR. For students learning English, for example, exposure to their target language—both oral and written—is the single most important factor in their language learning. SSR provides a nonthreatening way for students to learn new vocabulary and build their comprehension and fluency. And for many struggling readers who have never established a relationship with reading, learning to choose their own texts for SSR—establishing a bond with certain authors or particular genres—is uniquely empowering. They may need some help initially with choosing books that are appropriate for their reading skills, but once they get started, they are often amazed at their own improvement. Many students fear reading simply because it is something that they are constantly tested on, and, each time they "fail" it sends a message that makes them question their reading ability and even their intelligence. Often their "reading failure" stems from their attempts to tackle texts that are too difficult for them to comprehend. The same is true for us teachers; when we do not understand something (computer manuals, tax guidelines, complex legal agreements), we may become frustrated, lose interest, and even give up and shove the text to the side. We need to assure that our students don't get trapped in a cycle of failure—equating reading with a no-win, unpleasant experience. SSR enables students to choose texts that they can understand and are of interest them. An added benefit is that they are not tested, so they don't have to worry about memorizing details for a test! And, the more they read, the more engaged, efficient, skillful readers they become (Krashen, 2004). It's truly nothing short of miraculous. As Jan Pilgreen (2000) notes, "In-school free reading offers students opportunities to regain [or discover for the first time] the thrill of reading something for pure enjoyment and, more important, leads the way to more reading outside of school by offering accessible and stimulating materials that they can take with them" (p. 68).

Tips

Tips for Your Classroom:

Harnessing The Power of the Interactive Read-Aloud and Monitored SSR

The Read-Aloud

❖ Establish a predictable, consistent routine early in the school year with very clear expectations for the students.

❖ Choose from a wide variety of texts and introduce your students to a range of topics, authors, content areas, and genres.

❖ Model effective think-aloud strategies while you read.

❖ Don't be afraid to miscue while you read—show your students you are learning too.

❖ Have fun while you read aloud—pick texts you relish and demonstrate to students your love of reading.

❖ Invite student questions and comments; encourage active listening and verbal participation.

Tips for Your Classroom *(continued)*

Monitored SSR

❖ Establish a predictable, consistent routine early in the school year with very clear expectations for the students.

❖ Be consistent about the time of day you hold SSR and number of minutes you devote to it.

❖ Allow students to choose their own texts and do not test them on material.

❖ Create an in-class SSR library where students can share books.

❖ Hook your students on specific books with Book Talks; for indispensable guidance on effective Book Talks, don't miss *The Reading Zone* by Nancie Atwell (pp. 66–73; Scholastic, 2007).

❖ Monitor SSR; require students to keep track of the books they read as well as the authors and genres they explore; additionally, keep track of the number of pages they read and, at least once a week for students you know struggle with reading, find a way to check in and make sure they are actually understanding their books.

❖ Link SSR to explicit reading instruction.

❖ Create opportunities for students to share their favorites with each other in nonthreatening ways such as informal book talks, mini-reviews posted on a bulletin board, best-books lists with short annotations, posters, and so on.

❖ Encourage students, especially those who struggle with reading or are learning English, to listen to books on tape.

Chapter 6

CONNECTIVE READING AND WRITING:

Use the **Read-Aloud, Write-Aloud to Construct Meaning**

As noted throughout this book, the strategies we highlight are good for *all* learners. In this chapter, we discuss the importance of during-reading strategies. Essentially, we are pushing the read-aloud to the next level by using it to help students gain a deeper comprehension of text by connecting texts to their own writing. Reading and writing are inextricably linked because learners need to comprehend text through reading (or listening) in order to produce text via writing (or speaking). Therefore, when we are in schools and we hear teachers commenting on the fact that students are really struggling with their writing, we know that students are also likely struggling with their reading. For this reason, we recommend teaching reading and writing together to whatever extent that's possible; if you do so, you'll discover that your students have become more successful at both.

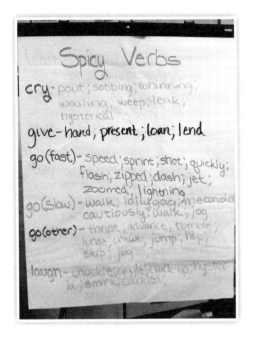

This chart was created by students and their teacher during a close reading of a short passage. Students in this class were making text-self connections and using writing to demonstrate their understanding of a text.

A *read-aloud, write-aloud* strategy weaves together the interactive read-aloud (a during-reading strategy) with writing (a post-reading strategy) to promote student comprehension of text. As you will see from the classroom example that follows, the writing that comes after the read-aloud does not necessarily need to apply directly to the content of the text, but it should certainly require that students employ comprehension strategies.

Link During-Reading Strategies With Post-Reading Strategies

As with the interactive read-aloud presented in Chapter 5, we cannot stress enough the importance of allowing kids the opportunity to show their thinking (Tovani, 2001) as they read in order to increase their level of comprehension. This is especially important for students who need assistance with checking their comprehension, such as struggling readers and students who have not yet grasped all the nuances of English.

During-reading strategies are often referred to as *fix-up strategies*, or techniques readers can tackle to monitor their comprehension. The term *fix-up* prompts us to think about what takes place when good readers get stuck. Unfortunately, for striving readers, "fixing-up" their reading often means stopping their reading altogether and giving up. Students must learn strategies to assist them with comprehension.

Table 6 shows several strategies that are commonly observed among good readers who are encountering comprehension problems. Before looking at the table, think about the challenges that cause you trouble when you are reading an unfamiliar text. When we discuss the kinds of texts that gave us problems in school, we assert that content-area textbooks were often difficult if we did not have enough background knowledge. As we have discussed in earlier chapters, the need for building background knowledge is essential to comprehension tasks (Wilhelm, Baker, & Dube, 2001). However, sometimes even a great deal of background knowledge is not enough! The good news is that if you teach students how to think through their comprehension difficulties, the challenge of even a complicated text can be somewhat mitigated.

Table 6	
Reader's Strategy	How It Is Accomplished
Identify main ideas	Highlight key words and phrases; annotate in margins; examine accompanying figures/pictures.
Self-monitor	Look at questions at the end of the section or chapter; create questions to check comprehension.
Clarify the assignment's purpose	Read subheadings of text; look for familiar vocabulary terms; review introduction to text (if content area book).

Closing the Achievement Gap

The goal of this chapter is to show how the comprehension strategies that the read-aloud promotes can get students to think about reading as writers. Once students begin to apply to their own writing some of the devices that they notice published authors using, they will have a much deeper understanding of the content of text. This greater ability to comprehend text will, in turn, positively affect their writing.

An important aspect of literacy development is the interaction of language input and language output. Typically, we think of *language input* as what we hear or read, and *language output* as what we say or write. We can also frame this as the *language we receive* and the *language we produce* (Padilla, 2006). When students are learning English, they need to receive language that they understand. As discussed in previous chapters, the comprehensibility of language input is essential for making meaning of texts. Prereading and during-reading strategies are often directly aimed at making the input of text more comprehensible. Cognitively, as students process the language they are receiving, they are working to make connections between what they already know and what is new. The strength of these connections determines the depth of students' comprehension.

There are different levels at which students make meaning of text. A basic level of comprehension might be gauged by whether or not students know all of the words in a given passage, while a higher level might be gauged by how students perform when they apply what they read to another situation. Student comprehension is deeper when they are successful in the latter. For example, asking your students a fact-based question about the content of the passage they just read (e.g., "When was the Montgomery bus boycott?") measures an entirely different level of comprehension than does giving them an application exercise (e.g., "Compare the events leading up to the Montgomery bus boycott to those preceding *Brown v. the Board of Education*.") Both the question and the exercise require students to process the content of the input (the text in this case) and produce an answer (either orally or in writing), but the latter produces writing that reveals the degree to which the students understood the text. It, unlike the fact-based question, requires students to make meaning of the text and then connect this meaning with other knowledge that they possess. Again, it is this connection that is the key to deepening student comprehension.

One great way to promote depth in student comprehension is to teach during-reading (input) strategies and postreading (output) strategies together. In this way, your students are challenged to craft the meaning of the passages they read into their own words and, in the process, commit the information to long-term memory where they are much more likely to retain it. Writing enables your students to explore their own ideas without the self-consciousness of speaking in public. Writing is also key for students learning English because it prompts them to handle a new lexicon as they move from reading to writing. This practice builds vocabulary and increases comprehension.

Effective Read-Aloud, Write-Aloud

We believe that reading aloud to secondary students is so important that we have already devoted an entire chapter to the topic. Middle and high school students, particularly those struggling with the language, often dread writing. As a result, teachers spend hours correcting grammar mistakes and trying to decipher meaning from poorly written student essays. Many teachers we know cite grading essays as their least favorite aspect of teaching. Most of the teachers who don't like reading student essays also concede that teaching writing is not their favorite thing, either.

To escape this nonproductive cycle, we offer a strategy that connects reading and writing in a nonthreatening manner and encourages students to think about reading as writers. At the most basic level, *read-aloud, write-aloud* is an opportunity to highlight the effective qualities of writing. And, it's a way to foster students' writing skills by focusing on specific aspects of their writing. For example, if you are trying to teach students how to write an interesting lead for their personal narrative, you might use a novel that you are reading aloud in order to give students an example of a strong lead from an accomplished author. Students cannot be expected to produce good writing if they are not exposed to good writing. Every writing skill you attempt to teach is best introduced through *mentor texts* which are outstanding books or pieces of writing, such as articles, instructional manuals, poetry, op-eds, and so on, that offer opportunities for teachers to highlight writing skills or conventions. Katie Wood Ray (2006) reminds us of the following:

"When teachers immerse students in reading and studying the kind of writing they want them to do, they are actually teaching on two levels. They teach students about the particular genre or writing that is the focus of the study, but they also teach students to use a habit of mind experienced writers use all the time. They teach them to read like writers (Ray, 1999, Smith, 1988), noticing as an insider how things are written. Students learn to look at texts the way a mechanic looks at cars or a musician listens to music, to use the particular knowledge system of a writer (Harste, 1992)."

The **View** from a Classroom

Let's listen in on an interactive read-aloud, write-aloud built around a mentor text—in this case, Chris Crutcher's *Deadline* (2007)—in Ms. Shaw's eleventh grade English classroom in a Houston, Texas urban school that is 62% Hispanic. Many of Ms. Shaw's students are non-native speakers, and in this particular class, a majority of the students are only recently out of ESL courses, so their academic language is still catching up with their social language. Students are required to pass an exit exam before graduating from high school, and many of the students Ms. Shaw teaches have great difficulty with the test. She teaches a broad array of students, from immigrant students who have just arrived from Mexico, to the sons and daughters of major league baseball players, to African-American students who moved to the area from New Orleans after Hurricane Katrina. Ms. Shaw's class represents a typical group of students in this school.

Ms. Shaw frequently uses read-aloud in her classes, but when her students are in the process of writing, she uses the read-aloud, write-aloud as a teaching tool to move beyond basic comprehension and towards skillful

(continued)

control. She notes that writing is perhaps the most daunting literacy skill her students face.

Recently, Ms. Shaw's students were writing personal narratives when she noticed as she was reviewing drafts of student writing that the leads seemed too "formulaic." In other words, they all started in the same dry and uninteresting way. The following exchange took place in her class in March:

Ms. Shaw: What do you think this book will be about? (She *holds up Chris Crutcher's* Deadline; *the cover features the picture of a boy standing on his head.*) Discuss your ideas with your neighbor for a minute.

(*Teacher gives students time to discuss as she walks around the room with the book showing the cover.*)

Vicki: It's probably about sports.

Ms. Shaw: Why do you say that?

Vicki: Well, we know Chris Crutcher writes about sports and the cover has a picture of a guy who looks athletic.

Ms. Shaw: Okay, good. What about you guys? (*She points to another group of students.*)

Pablo: We think the boy is going to be a misfit athlete, because he is standing on his head. Something ain't right about him.

Ms. Shaw: Possibly. I like the way you all are using the artwork on the cover to predict what the book will be about. Okay, I am going to read you just the first paragraph, and I want you to really pay attention to how the writer grabs the reader. (*She reads the paragraph to the class.*)

Early August

(continued)

My plan was to focus my senior year on information I could use after graduation when I set out for Planet Earth from the Pluto that is Trout, Idaho, population 943. My SATs said I wasn't even close to brain-dead and I was set to be accepted at any college I chose, as long as I chose one that would accept me. A lot of guys use their senior year to coast; catch up on partying and reward themselves for making it this far. Not me. This was my year to read everything I could get my hands on, to speak up, push myself and my teachers to get the true hot poop on the World At Large, so I could hit the ground running. How big of a pain in the ass do you think that would make me?

Ms. Shaw: . . . What kinds of things did the writer do to get the reader's attention?

Marta: He doesn't really tell you too much. He tells you just enough to get you interested in reading more.

Ryan: Yeah, like, in the opening paragraph, he, like, makes everything all dramatic. Like, he starts out by saying the kid has only a little time left on this earth.

Ms. Shaw: Let's look at the language for a second. I'm going to give you a copy of the text and I want you to look at it with your group and notice the author's word choice.

(*Ms. Shaw passes out papers and students talk at tables.*)

Ms. Shaw: So, how would you characterize his language?

Jamie: We think it was kind of forceful, or dramatic, like the other group said.

Rita: Well, we think he used certain words to make us think.

(continued)

Ms. Shaw: Okay, so you think he used forceful language to make the reader think?

Jamie: Yes. I mean, he could have just used more easygoing words.

Ms. Shaw: So, authors should be careful about the words they choose?

Jamie: Of course!

Ms. Shaw: Isn't that how your personal narrative should read? Shouldn't the opening make the reader want to continue reading? I want you to get with a partner and share your opening paragraph of your essay, and then have your partner predict what the essay will be about. I'll bet you can improve the beginning of your essay this way.

(Students spend time in groups while Ms. Shaw works her way around the classroom checking in with each pair.)

Ms. Shaw: Okay, you all are used to doing write-alouds. Today I have a treat for you—I found my personal narrative from when I was applying to college, and brought it in to share with you.

Jamie: You had to do the same thing when you were a senior?

Ms. Shaw: Of course. And believe it or not, that was not that long ago. I'm not that old.

(There are a few giggles and some whispering. Ms. Shaw puts up an overhead with the opening paragraph of her personal narrative.)

Okay, let's read this together. (*She reads the paragraph aloud.*) As you can see, I was writing to the same prompt that all of you are writing to. And as you can see, this paragraph can use some improvement.

(continued)

Brian:	Yeah. This essay was good enough to get you into University of Texas? I think even mine is better.
Ms. Shaw:	Thanks, Brian. I appreciate that. (*Students laugh and wait for a comeback from Brian.*) Actually, though, you are right . . . a lot of you have some good ideas for your essays. Let's look at this paragraph and improve it together. I want to write like Chris Crutcher.

(*Long silence while students look at the paragraph on the screen. Ms. Shaw draws a line under the paragraph and begins to rewrite the first sentence.*)

	Come on, help me out. A lot of you had good ideas in your groups for improving your opening sentences.
Marta:	I think, maybe, instead of starting that way, you should start with the second sentence. I mean, you say the same thing kind of in both sentences.
Noe:	Yeah, maybe you could start with the idea that going to college was really your dad's idea.
Ms. Shaw:	Okay, I like that idea. How should I say it?
Marta:	Just like that—"College was really my dad's idea."
Brian:	What if you use the quote that you use farther down—the one about school is your future? That is like, kind of more forceful . . . like in the book.
Ms. Shaw:	I like these ideas. (*She begins to write, "My dad always told me . . . " and then stops.*) Wait, how about this?

(*The lesson continues with the class helping Ms. Shaw fix up her introduction.*)

Read-Aloud, Write-Aloud With Purpose

In the first part of the lesson, Ms. Shaw did two things that are keys to her success. First, she took the opportunity to show students how reading and writing are connected. She began by telling the students that she knew they could craft brighter, livelier writing. Then, she introduced the mentor text (Chris Crutcher's *Deadline*) inviting her students to make predictions first about what they expected to hear before she began reading to them. Finally, she focused on the lead, showing them how an interesting lead makes the reader want to continue reading the writer's words.

In the Classroom

Invite professional authors to your classroom to talk with your students about their own writing process. In this way, your students will come to understand that the nature of writing is hard work—it takes tremendous commitment, discipline, and practice. Most authors will explain that writing is not easy for them, that they have to work hard at it, logging hours every day. But, ultimately, they also note how amazingly gratifying writing can be. By getting a glimpse into the lives of professional writers, students learn a lot about themselves and their own perspectives on writing. Most important, they learn that writing, like every other skill they might tackle, requires hard work and lots and lots and practice.

Notice how Ms. Shaw keeps probing the students for the information she is trying to get across: word choice matters. We believe she owes her success to the fact that she copies the text and lets the students work with the text in a real way. The students know what they have to do without having to do a worksheet about "vivid verbs" or some other grammar topic that likely would not produce the same effect in the student's subsequent drafts.

One can't help but notice how purposeful Ms. Shaw is in allowing students to engage with one another during this lesson. This is so important for struggling readers and students learning English because it opens the affective filter (Crawford & Krashen, 2007) that enables students to be receptive to learning. She could have called on students to answer her prediction questions, but instead, Ms. Shaw allows the students to work in self-selected groups. She believes that the more comfortable students are in class, the more likely they are to learn. Ms. Shaw's assumption is in line with Krashen's (1982) belief that learning must take place in a nonthreatening environment to guard against affective filter shut-off. All of us can remember times when we have been in situations that were uncomfortable, and we felt threatened. Our natural response to threat is to shut down. Allowing students an opportunity to "check their answers" with peers makes perfect sense. At every stage of this lesson, Ms. Shaw allows students to work with a partner before sharing with the class. Some teachers are opposed to this type of classroom practice because it almost seems like cheating. School seems to be the only place on the planet where collaboration is viewed as cheating! But make no mistake—Ms. Shaw later evaluates each student independently on the final product, the rewritten lead. Many of the most successful organizations rely on team collaboration to produce a quality product. Even in our own profession, we are encouraged to collaborate with other teachers so that our lesson plans are more effective, helping to guarantee stronger student achievement.

The text that Ms. Shaw chooses to read is purposeful. Chris Crutcher is a Young Adult novelist who writes compelling leads, but he is also an author who appeals to a wide group of students. She could just as easily read the beginning of *The Scarlet Letter* by Nathaniel Hawthorne. This classic of American literature has a phenomenal lead, but Mrs. Shaw knows her students and understands that this particular class is not able to relate to Hawthorne's vocabulary and complex sentence structures. Remember, this class is a mixed-ability class with a large number of non-native English speakers. Demonstrating effective writing with Young Adult literature that features vocabulary kids are used to hearing is more likely to engage and interest students. Another characteristic of Crutcher's books is that they represent a variety of personalities. While the characters are usually Caucasian or African American, the personalities of the characters are universal. Crutcher is by no means the only Young Adult author who has a loyal following! There are many, many authors who write for young adults who are equally engaging.

Young Adult Authors Reluctant Readers Love

Chris Crutcher: *Chinese Handcuffs, Whale Talk, Deadline, Staying Fat for Sarah Byrnes*

Sharon M. Draper: *Tears of a Tiger*

Gail Giles: *Right Behind You*

S. E. Hinton: *The Outsiders*

Cynthia Lord: *Rules*

Walter Dean Myers: *Monster*

Rodman Philbrick: *Freak the Mighty*

Luis J. Rodriguez: *Always Running*

J.K. Rowling: *Harry Potter* series

Louis Sachar: *Holes*

Jerry Spinelli: *Maniac Magee, The Egg*

Alan Sitomer: *Homeboyz, The Secret Story of Sonia Rodriguez, The Hoopster*

Paul Zindel: *The Pigman*

Using Write-Aloud

The combination of the read-aloud with write-aloud is especially potent because it capitalizes on students' comprehension strategies and incorporates a level of application where students not only have to process the meaning of the text but are also encouraged to read as writers. This is a very challenging task for students, but precise, direct connections between reading and writing can prove especially beneficial. For example, Ms. Shaw frames her discussion of Crutcher's voice around the concept of creating effective lead sentences. If her focus was too general, such as a discussion of voice in the novel, she likely would have lost a number of students.

For the write-aloud itself, many of the same principles apply as with read-aloud. The goal is to make your thinking about writing transparent by taking the time to write with your students. Physically writing on the board (or on an overhead or smart board) is key because students need to see you in the act. They need to be a part of your process as you think through your writing. Ms. Shaw makes a great decision to bring in one of her essays from when she was at the same stage as her students, because it personalizes the experience and demonstrates that, as a high school senior, she was not a perfect writer. As Ms. Shaw shares her own struggles to learn, she helps her students revalue their own learning processes and also helps them appreciate the nature of learning—which necessarily entails risk taking, which often leads to missteps. The goal for students when they do make mistakes is to track what went wrong, understand the thinking behind the missteps, and move on as stronger, more knowledgeable, and more capable learners.

In the Classroom

Produce a class newsletter. Regardless of your content area, the creation of a newsletter (or newspaper, book, journal, and so on) that showcases the writing of students in your class can be a rewarding endeavor. You can focus the content of the newsletter on a specific unit of study, an event, or simply "Writings from Room 309." The idea is to encourage students to work hard on one piece of writing that they want to publish. Too often, students see writing as communication solely between student and teacher. This should not be the case, and students need to experience the joys of publishing, understand the process, and access opportunities to publish their work for a larger audience. For information about online publishing—creating digital books in any language that can be shared with a global audience of young readers and writers around the world—go to www.RealeBooks.com.

You do not need to bring in your college essays to make the write-aloud work. Instead, you simply need to get in the habit of writing with your students and making your thinking about writing transparent. Step inside your own writing process and invite your students to accompany you (Graves & Kittle, 2005). You need to have a clear purpose for the writing that you do with them, and you need to be willing to make mistakes on the way to showing them that writing is a process that you learn and improve upon. You need to regard writing as not simply good or bad or something only a few talented people can produce. Show them that writing is a remarkable tool for both learning and expression that all students can develop. Your students will learn this lesson most effectively if you routinely demonstrate working on your own writing in front of them and thinking out loud as you do it—cracking open your writing process for your students so they understand the range of decisions you make at both a global level (topic choice, genre, voice) and particular level (word choice, punctuation, grammar, and so on).

For our purposes here, and for the goal of using write-aloud as an effective literacy strategy in your classroom, we encourage you to link it with read-aloud to push students' cognitive connections to text one step further. You are constantly receiving written work from your students. Read-aloud, write-aloud enables you to see your students' abilities as writers as being connected to their abilities as readers. Again, as we hope we've made clear, by teaching reading using key mentor texts to highlight examples from the "masters", you will be helping to improve your students' writing.

Tips

Tips for Your Classroom:
Improving Your Students' Reading Through Writing

Read-Aloud, Write-Aloud

❖ Follow tips for effective read-aloud (see Chapter 5).

❖ Identify a particular literary element or writing skill that your students need to learn.

❖ Select mentor texts that showcase the writing element or skill you want to teach.

❖ Introduce students to *reading as writers* by highlighting and discussing specific features of the mentor text.

❖ Focus on your specific writing objective in each mentor text.

❖ Encourage students to discuss the author's style and key features of a mentor text. What do they notice? What works for them and why? What doesn't work as well and why?

❖ Use the mentor text and students' own writing together, and move back and forth between the two, comparing and contrasting.

❖ Encourage students to work with each other on their respective writing and provide opportunities for them to share their writing with the whole class.

Write-Aloud

❖ Choose academic writing language that you will concentrate on for the year (e.g., introduction, voice, lead, literary elements, conventions, conclusion, and so on).

❖ Use your own writing (show students you are an active writer).

❖ Demonstrate through a write-aloud the ways in which you go about crafting your writing.

❖ Take the risks necessary for real learning, which means you will then naturally make mistakes; discuss your stumbles with your students; model how you learn from your mistakes and grow as a writer.

❖ Encourage students to lead a write-aloud for the class with their own writing.

Chapter 7

UNDERSTANDING THROUGH ASKING:

Engage ALL Learners with Active Questioning Strategies

Perhaps the most difficult challenge facing teachers today is to engage all students all the time. The idea of cooperative learning is appealing to students because they get to work with their peers. The idea also appeals to teachers because it takes some of the responsibility for learning off their shoulders and places it with the students, where the responsibility belongs. If cooperative learning is structured properly, it is almost guaranteed to engage students.

As we discussed in Chapter 3, the best reason to use any cooperative learning strategy is that these activities assist students in processing information. Teachers who dislike cooperative learning often cite a lack of student initiative. For this reason, we believe that teachers will be most successful if they first engage students in learning and only then send them off for a cooperative learning experience or an independent learning activity. In our experience, instruction is most successful when students grasp the concepts at hand before the teacher releases them to practice on their own. When we visit classrooms, perhaps the most common mistake we see new teachers make is one in which the teacher opens a lesson with a great presentation, releases the students to independent practice immediately after, and then watches things fall apart.

In the Classroom

U se "exit tickets" to encourage active questioning. Collecting informal feedback from students at the end of class in the form of an exit ticket is good practice. Not only do you provide students with the opportunity to reflect upon and showcase what they have (or have not) learned, but you are also getting vital information about their levels of understanding. As a questioning strategy, you can use an exit slip on which you ask students to write down one question that they have about the material from that day. You can even make this process a routine and reward students for deeper-level questions. Your goal is to get students to ask questions, as opposed to getting them to give answers (see Appendix C on page 138 for an example of an exit ticket).

For example, when Shawn first taught high school English, he had one class of eleventh grade students who were in a class called Sheltered English III. This class was for students who had been in ESL courses for the maximum amount of time allowed by law. The ESL students now had to be mainstreamed into regular classes, and to add insult to injury, they were required to pass the state assessment given at the end of that year in order to get a high school diploma. This was high-stakes testing at its most absurd. Shawn was supposed to teach these ESL students the standard high school curriculum, which, at the time, centered on novels such as *The Great Gatsby* and *The Scarlet Letter*. The previous year, most of his ESL students had been reading *Clifford, the Big Red Dog*, so he wasn't at all convinced of their ability to tackle these classics of American literature.

After many frustrating attempts to do what he thought he was supposed to do, Shawn decided to do the right thing for his kids and help them improve their reading skills. They were studying the Holocaust. He decided they would read *The Wave* by Todd Strasser, a novel about a teacher who conducted an experiment with his class in order to demonstrate the tragedy of the Holocaust. The book discusses Hitler at length, and, naively, Shawn believed his students possessed the background information about Hitler to process the text. After all, Hitler is perhaps the most infamous person in history.

While reading the book, Shawn would dutifully divide the class into groups and give assignments for "literature circle" in order to motivate students to read. He became frustrated because students did not seem to understand the main points of the book. They could not complete the assignments he gave them, and he falsely assumed that they were not taking the assignment or the class seriously. Finally, one student raised her hand and said, "Mr., we are trying, but we just don't get it." Upon further questioning, Shawn discovered that they did not know who Hitler was! He was astounded and embarrassed all at the same time—embarrassed, that is, at his own lack of awareness.

This was a defining moment for Shawn as a teacher. He realized that he failed not only to build background knowledge (a cardinal sin—especially for an English teacher), but that he further failed to question students enough to gauge their understanding of the material before he sent them to work in their groups. Of course, the groups were not productive and he had nobody to blame but himself.

We often retell this story to teachers and student teachers to illustrate the importance of prereading. However, the story does more than make the case for prereading; it shows that teachers can also have a positive impact on students' reading comprehension skills by asking questions *during* the lesson. Teachers need to ask more questions of their students in a variety of ways to make sure students are processing new concepts.

A discussion of questioning strategies isn't complete without a discussion of the taxonomies of questioning. Of course, we all remember Bloom's Taxonomy from our education classes in college. Following is a brief review:

Table 7	
Bloom's Taxonomy	
Synthesis	Highest level of critical thinking
Evaluation	
Analysis	
Application	
Comprehension	
Knowledge	Lowest level of critical thinking

Research indicates that most teacher-generated exams and in-class questioning reside at the lowest level of this questioning taxonomy. In order to push our students to higher levels of critical thinking, we must begin to ask questions in the higher level of the taxonomy (i.e. knowledge). Think about one of your last class sessions in which you questioned students to determine whether or not they understood the material. Where did your questions fall in the taxonomy hierarchy? Table 8 contains some sample questions from an eighth grade history class. (Note that the teacher gives this lesson on the electoral process before she received training on asking higher-level questions.)

Table 8 shows that the teacher's questions remain, for the most part, at the lowest taxonomy level. She is reviewing questions her students will encounter on a quiz they are scheduled to take the next day. Clearly, students will be asked to demonstrate only minimal knowledge of the electoral process.

Table 8
Question
How many electoral college votes are necessary to win the Presidential election?
Who said the following: "Today, our long national nightmare has ended"?
In what year was George W. Bush elected?
What are three core beliefs of both the Republican and Democratic parties?

In the Classroom

Get your students involved in the questions you use to assess them. After reading a section of text with your students, ask them, "What would be a good question to ask to see if you understood this section of the text?" Have students respond orally at first, and then ask, "Why is that a good question?" Begin a discussion about fact-based and application questions. Continue asking students to form application questions on their own. To take this to the next level, have students submit what they think are good test questions to assess their understanding of the text (or other unit of study). Tell them that you will use some of their questions on the test. This is a great way for them to study for the test and for you to gauge their understanding before an assessment.

In the Classroom

Focus on verbs that help ask good questions. Post Bloom's taxonomy in your classroom. In reviewing the purpose of the taxonomy, ask students questions about a text you are working with, and have them place the questions on one level of the taxonomy. Write the question and the taxonomy level on the board. Next, have students underline the verb in the question. As you move to deeper levels of the taxonomy, students will notice that the verbs change (instead of forms of *to be* or *to do*, verbs like *explain*, *describe*, and *choose* appear). Write down these key verbs in their respective levels of the taxonomy, and urge students to ask themselves questions using these verbs.

There is nothing wrong with asking knowledge-level questions. Indeed it is important to know basic information about a topic before you can expand on it and go deeper. The point is, however, that some of our questions need to delve deeper into the subject matter so that our students can make the complex connections that lead to learning that lasts. Put another way, consider the difference between a cook and a chef. Anyone who can read can be a cook, because if you can read basic directions, you can follow them and create a meal. A chef, however, is someone who has studied and experimented more and understands difficult concepts like how to layer flavors in recipes and how spices and seasonings will react with each other. We can think of questioning in a similar way. It is better to ask our students probing questions so that they can do more than follow a simple recipe.

Being aware of the questions you plan to ask enables you to practice more effective questioning techniques. Take, for example, the teacher who asks the basic-level questions that appear in Table 8. She underwent some questioning-strategy training and was taught about the different levels of questioning. Then, with the help of colleagues who were also trained, she began to *rethink* the types of questions she had asked in her lesson. When asked to revisit the quiz review, she came up with the questions that appear in Table 9:

Table 9	
Questions	Level
Explain the electoral college process and discuss its advantages and disadvantages.	Evaluation
What is the significance of the following quote: "Today, our long national nightmare has ended"?	Application
Describe the mood of the country in the year 2000 that led to the victory of George W. Bush.	Application
Choose one core belief of either the Democratic or Republican party and describe what circumstances led to the belief being adopted as a core value.	Synthesis

Note that the questions are more difficult the second time around, as they require students to demonstrate true understanding of the content in order to get the correct answer. Additionally, there was a greater variety in the questions. While the more thought-provoking questions do not lend themselves to a Scantron test, students who can answer questions that inspire real thinking, will have truly learned something beyond just the basic facts.

Incorporating Questioning Into Instruction

So how do we manage to incorporate more challenging questions into our classroom instruction on a daily basis? One technique, which we call 3PQ (Three-Part Questioning) will help you not only to ask better questions but it will also model the reading process for students. 3PQ gets its name from the three phases of questioning that it encourages students to use: questioning *before* reading, questioning *during* reading, and questioning *after* reading. Here are the steps you can take to implement this strategy, followed by a model of the strategy:

Steps for Implementation

1. Choose a small piece of text (newspaper articles work great for this strategy).
2. Choose a small group of students with mixed ability levels.
3. Preview the text with students.
4. Predetermine, with student input, where you will stop for comprehension checks.
5. Determine how you will read the text (teacher read-aloud, group members taking turns, and so on).
6. Read the text.
7. Pose follow-up questions, connections.

The **View** from a Classroom

3PQ in Action

Ms. Lee teaches middle school science in Houston, Texas. She strives to make the content of her course relevant to her students' lives by connecting it to current events and, to that end, she continually uses multiple sources of text to encourage students to read about topics from different perspectives (Nichols, 2009). Ms. Lee teaches in a school that serves grades 6–8. The student population is close to being equally mixed among African-American, Latino, and Caucasian students. The segment of the lesson below comes from a seventh grade classroom in April. Ms. Lee has set up classroom centers where student groups (most consist of four students) work quietly on a self-contained task. While other groups work on their own, Ms. Lee works with one group at the reading table in the back of the room. The text Ms. Lee chose for this day was an article from the *Houston Chronicle* (found on the following pages and precedes the actual lesson).

Cancer Patient Had Salmonella Prior to Death

Wife of man says husband fell ill days after eating tomato-based food

By Allan Turner (2008)

Not on the Menu
Many of the nation's most popular restaurant chains have stopped serving most types of raw tomatoes.

McDonald's
The chain has stopped serving sliced tomatoes on its sandwiches. It will continue serving grape tomatoes in its salads because no problems have been linked to that variety.

Outback
The parent company of Outback Steakhouse and Carrabba's stopped serving all raw tomatoes other than grape tomatoes. The company also instructed restaurants to discard salsa containing raw tomatoes.

Burger King
The company has withdrawn raw round red tomatoes from most of its U.S. restaurants.

Also withdrawing tomatoes
Yum Brands: Taco Bell, KFC, Long John Silver's, A&W All-American Food

Darden Restaurants: Red Lobster, Olive Garden

Chipotle Mexican Grill

Source: Associated Press

Health officials Monday confirmed that a Houston cancer patient who died after being hospitalized with nausea, diarrhea and high fever had contracted Saintpaul salmonellosis, but stopped short of saying the debilitating illness caused his death.

Salmonella Saintpaul—thought spread by eating some types of raw tomatoes—has sickened 146 people in 16 states. Confirmation that Raul Rivera, 67, also had contracted the disease brings the total of Harris County victims to 15. Fifty-seven Texans have been sickened by the disease.

City health department spokeswoman Kathy Barton said Rivera's death certificate officially attributed his death to lymphoma, a cancer of the lymphatic system. But, she added, salmonella poisoning, extremely dangerous for infants, the elderly and cancer patients and others with a depressed immune system, was a contributing factor.

Rivera is thought to be the first person to die in the current outbreak.

Rivera's wife, Barbara, said her husband ate tomatoes during a restaurant meal celebrating good news he had received concerning his cancer treatment. Four other family members who ate tomatoes also became ill.

Meanwhile, McDonalds and Taco Bell joined other restaurant chains in deleting tomatoes from their menus. The U.S. Food and Drug Administration has urged consumers to avoid raw Roma, plum and red round tomatoes until the source of the outbreak has been determined.

Cherry, grape and homegrown tomatoes, as well as those sold still attached to the vine, are believed safe.

The FDA said that tomatoes commercially grown in Texas and seven other states do not appear to be the source of contamination.

Florida, which produces about half the nation's commercial tomatoes, has not been cleared. Last year, Florida and Virginia—linked to most of 12 tomato-related salmonella outbreaks in the past decade—were enrolled in a special FDA safety initiative to ensure good food production and handling practices.

Reggie Brown, manager of the Florida Tomato Committee, a trade group, could not be reached for comment Monday.

Barbara Rivera said her husband joined family members in a celebratory meal at a local Mexican restaurant in late May after he was told there was new hope he would survive his cancer. Rivera had already undergone eight chemotherapy and 14 radiation treatments and most of his tumors had shrunk.

Rivera's wife said her husband and four other family members ate pico de gallo, a tomato-based condiment. Two days later Rivera began suffering nausea and diarrhea. For several days he was treated at home with pain relievers and liquids. He was admitted to a hospital six days after the meal.

Rivera died Wednesday. The four others also became ill, Barbara Rivera said, but didn't require hospitalization.

Salmonella Saintpaul—one of 2,500 strains of the bacterium—is relatively rare, the U.S. Centers for Disease Control and Prevention said. Of 1.4 million salmonell osis cases last year, slightly more than 400 involved the Saintpaul strain.

Nationwide, only about three cases of the Saintpaul strain were reported in the first six months of 2007.

The CDC, however, estimated that 38 unreported cases occur for every instance brought to the attention of a physician. (p. A-2)

Ms. Lee: Today we are going to read an article from the paper about something we have been studying in class. All of you have heard about the recent outbreak of salmonella, right? Who can tell me what salmonella is?

Billie: It is a disease you get from food and it kills you.

Ms. Lee: Okay, does it always kill you?

Billie: Most of the time.

Ms. Lee: Well, you are correct . . . salmonella is a food-borne disease that can be deadly in some cases; however, most of the time, it's not deadly. Does anyone know how you can get salmonella?

A number of students reply: From tomatoes!

Ms. Lee: That is the most recent cause, but did you know you can also get it from raw or undercooked chicken?

Sylvia: I just know that McDonald's is not serving tomatoes right now because some guy recently died from eating tomatoes.

Ms. Lee: You are correct. It's not just McDonald's that isn't serving tomatoes right now. The article we are going to read will help us learn more about this disease. Today, the four of us are going to read an article from the *Houston Chronicle*. (*teacher distributes copies of the article*)

Ms. Lee: We know the topic of the article is salmonella, based on the discussion we have been having, right? Okay, this is a newspaper article, so what should we do before we start reading?

(continued)

Sandra: We should look at the title of the article and the headings.

Ms. Lee: Good. Why should we look at those things?

Sandra: Well, it will give us a good idea of what we are going to read about.

Ms. Lee: Good! Okay, so I am going to give you a sheet of paper to record your thinking on while we read this article from the *Houston Chronicle*. I want you to all take a few minutes and fill out Part 1 of the handout: *What I think the text is about*.

Ms. Lee: Now that you have had a chance to do so, let's talk about it for a minute. Who would like to share their answers?

Juan: I think the story is going to be about someone who dies from salmonella, but they had cancer first. The title of the article says so.

Ms. Lee: Good. Does everyone agree?

(*Students nod, but otherwise there is silence.*)

Ms. Lee: Okay, let's begin reading. I think today I will read out loud to you and we will stop when needed in order to ask questions.

Ms. Lee: (*reading aloud*) "'Not on the Menu'. Many of the nation's most popular restaurant chains have stopped serving most types of raw tomatoes."

Ms. Lee: (*after pausing*) What are "restaurant chains?"

Sylvia: You know, the popular places—McDonalds, Burger King, Wendy's.

Juan: Jack in the Box, IHOP . . .

Ms. Lee: Okay, Okay, I get it. But what is the difference between a chain and just a regular old restaurant?

(continued)

(*Silence . . . wait time*)

Billie: There are a lot of them. Like, they are all over the place.

Sandra: Yeah, they are all owned by some bigger company.

Ms. Lee: Okay, good. So the question I want you to start thinking about is, why is it important that the restaurant chains, as opposed to all restaurants, have stopped serving tomatoes?

(*Silence*)

Ms. Lee: You don't have to know now, but I want you to keep it in mind as you read. Oh yeah, by the way, why are they only stopping service of *raw* tomatoes?

Billie: I think, because, when you cook them, they are cleaner.

Sylvia: Yeah, you get the bacteria off of 'em when you cook 'em . . . .

(*The lesson continues with Ms. Lee's read-aloud. She continues to ask questions on her own and use the 3PQ handout.*)

Why 3PQ Works

In the preceding View from a Classroom, Ms. Lee leads her students to be active readers. She captures their interest in the text before they read it by connecting the text with their personal experiences. She asks lots of leading questions in order to guide their reading, and she reads the text to them so that they can follow along and focus on comprehension. Alternatively, she could ask for volunteers to read the text. This would be okay, except struggling readers in the group could have difficulty with comprehension because they are often too worried about the performance aspect of reading aloud. By reading aloud, Ms. Lee models good reading behaviors. For example, she stops at several places to check for comprehension and she does a think-aloud for the students. Perhaps the best thing that Ms. Lee does is to provide kids with a place to record their thinking as they read.

3PQ

Student Name: _____

Directions: Use this handout to record your thoughts as you work through the text.

Part I: What I Think the Text Is About
Look at the title. What are your predictions and questions?
Look at the subject headings. What are your predictions and questions?

Part II: Notes While Reading
List any vocabulary words that you don't know and tell what you think the word means based on the context in which it is used:
Word   Page#   I think it means . . .

Part III: Conclusions
I think the main idea(s) of the text are . . .

I have the following questions . . .

While this handout is simple, it will definitely help you to get students to express their thinking and ask questions while they read. This is what we want all readers to do. The simplicity of this strategy also enables you to continue to develop these questioning techniques with your students. While you model effective questioning during your read-aloud, you can assess how your students handle questions of varying levels, and push them towards deeper comprehension through more effective questioning. You can also discuss questions with your students, and begin to reinforce their use of higher-order questioning by reviewing their handouts with them and encouraging them (through praise, grades, extra credit, and so forth) to use questions that fall into the synthesis, analysis, and evaluation phases of Bloom's Taxonomy.

Why 3PQ Works with Struggling Readers

Making questioning an explicit process during reading helps all students become better readers. For students learning English and students who are struggling with their reading, questioning can be an exceptionally powerful strategy because it reveals that there are different pathways to meaning. By the time they reach middle school and high school, struggling readers are often so frustrated by the prospect of reading long or complex texts that they give up before they even try. This is when we often hear them say, mechanically, *I don't get it*. As frustrating as this may be for us as teachers to hear, it is usually intensified one hundredfold for the student. What we have found is that the *it* in the phrase, "I don't get it" is something that can take on very different meaning for student and teacher.

For struggling readers, *it* most often refers to *the right answer*. For decades, both teachers and students have been programmed to focus on the one right answer. However, when it comes to reading comprehension, we know that there are many different right answers. We all approach what we read from different perspectives, we have different background knowledge, values, objectives, and often, different linguistic and cultural understandings. While we are reading, we make different connections to the content we are reading, and these connections shape how we interpret the text. A great example for us, as English teachers, is to think about the (literally) dozens of times we have read *Romeo and Juliet*. The experience of reading the play for the first time, as sixteen-year-olds, was markedly different than it is when we read it, now, as highly educated adults. Not only do we notice different lines, feel differently about certain characters, and forge new connections to current events, but we also draw new meanings from the play and feel new emotions after the final scene.

Many students don't read anything more than once because they don't see the value of rereading if they "don't get it" the first time. They don't read on their own (for pleasure) because reading at school is a chore. And they certainly don't think of reading as an experience. In large part, this is because many students regard reading as yet another typical school assignment that centers on searching for the right answer. As frustrating as this cycle is, it is easy to stop.

In the Classroom

To focus on the importance of deeper-level questioning, make the process explicit by using the same text at different points in the marking period. A letter to the editor or a critical book review often work well, but you can choose any text, really. During the first reading, ask mostly knowledge-level questions, and dig for students' overall reactions to the piece. For the second reading (preferably after a unit of study on related material), ask students deeper-level, application questions. This will give students the opportunity to apply their new knowledge to a text they are familiar with. Additionally, it will show them that reading and questioning are cumulative processes that grow with new knowledge—just because we read something doesn't mean that we know it and are done with it.

Active reading is one key to stopping this cycle, and questioning is the best tool to use while actively reading. What we cannot do is assume that students know how to effectively use questioning to comprehend text. Again, they are so accustomed to looking for the one right answer that we have to stop them, ask them to make predictions about what they are reading, and then model effective questioning. The 3PQ is a perfect strategy to begin with because it is easy for students to do and it provides a structure for the questioning strategies that you will develop with them. The handout models effective questions (about predictions and summarizing) and encourages students to think of questions of their own. You will likely find that when students first start using 3PQ they form questions that draw them to the right answer. (When writing questions about the title, for example, they will often write, "What is this about?" or "Why did the author use this title?") However, as you teach them to use a variety of questions, and show them how you question what you read while doing read-aloud, you will notice that students start to ask more provocative questions; for example, they might ask about using a specific word in the title, or inquire how this title relates to an earlier section in the book.

The potential that awaits students once they begin to realize that there is *no one right answer* to everything they read is tremendous. Especially for struggling readers, questioning can answer the always present question, Why do we have to read this? If you can approach this question with honesty and transparency through effective modeling and instruction, you can start to show your students that their inclination to question is good. Some questions are better than others, but the process is important. For success in reading, your students need to learn how to effectively ask questions while they are reading. You can do this, and 3PQ can help you.

Tips

Tips for Your Classroom:

Encouraging Students to Question While Reading

There is no one right answer

❖ Make sure students know what they are about to read and why they are reading it.

❖ When students ask "Why do we have to read this?" take the time to recognize their inclination to question and use this question as a way to prepare them to read and make connections to other course content.

3PQ

❖ Choose a small piece of text (newspaper articles work great for this strategy).

❖ Choose a small group of students with mixed ability levels.

❖ Preview the text with students.

❖ Predetermine, with student input, where you will stop for comprehension checks.

❖ Determine how you will read the text (teacher read-aloud, group members taking turns, and so on).

❖ Read the text.

❖ Address follow-up questions and connections.

Part 3

Closing Thoughts

In *Dead Poet's Society* (Shulman, 1989), Mr. Keating says to his students: "Life is a powerful play that goes on and you may contribute a verse. What will your verse be?" . . . . When we connect books and students we live meaningful lives and we show students how they can live meaningful lives. It is never too late to make those connections. With each memory of a positive reading experience, we give the generative gift that lasts for lifetimes. We give them friends, wisdom, answers, and hope. We give them mentors —mentors who will be there long after we are gone.

> —Janet Allen, It's Never Too Late: Leading
>   Adolescents to Lifelong Literacy

Chapter 8

A CALL FOR ACTION:

What it Takes to **Close** the Achievement Gap

William Shakespeare captures a simple truth— "ripeness is all." When we discuss the current state of public education in the United States, we must acknowledge the fact that our schools are ripe for change, ripe for innovation, ripe for becoming truly great. We cannot hesitate because the information age is upon us, and access to knowledge is more readily available than ever before. The world is becoming connected in a way that invites everyone to learn about the most foreign of lands, people, and ideas. The time is here for us as educators to make sure that all students have the abilities to access all that surrounds them. And this quest starts in the classroom.

In this book, we contend that an asset approach to student learning is a significant first step in the quest for student success. The asset approach is a simple idea. Indeed, it may be what originally drew us to teaching—we love kids and want to help them succeed. Sadly, the current educational approach in most schools is to overlook students' strengths and to focus, instead, on their weaknesses. And, as a nation, we seem obsessed with "problems," real or imagined, that impact American public education—our international standings on test scores, a lack of teacher accountability, and an overall craze for standardized testing. Additionally, the system has become so focused on remediation that student strengths often go unnoticed and untapped.

This deficit approach is especially detrimental for students of color. Instructional methods used in most secondary classrooms continue to focus primarily on the methods that have traditionally worked for Caucasian students, so, to succeed academically, students of color are forced to "beat the odds" (Cabrera & Padilla, 2004). The achievement gap is growing (Darling-Hammond, 2007). We need look no further than historical data provided by the U.S. Department of Education related to NAEP testing. These scores have remained flat since 1970, largely because we have not changed our instructional methods to meet the changing demographics of our public schools (Bird, 2005). Furthermore, immigrant students are forced to assimilate linguistically and culturally if they are to achieve. In essence, students of color are set up for failure. And it is not only students who become occluded by fear—teachers suffer as well. Jackson (2001) argues that fear is the main cause for the achievement gap in our schools. She writes that, "teachers are under all kinds of pressure, but the one they articulate the most emotionally is fear . . . most poignantly fear of not being able to reach their culturally different students to reverse underachievement" (1–2).

Considering the tremendous growth in the number of students of color and the projections for this growth to continue in the decades to come (Darling-Hammond, 2007), the time truly is ripe to change our focus in schools. An asset approach is one way to begin this change in schools. Instead of fearing your students or fearing your abilities to reach them, please keep the word "asset" in mind as you reflect on your teaching. In this book we provide numerous examples of your students' strengths as learners and your strengths as teachers. Keep these strengths in mind as you set up your classroom, plan your lessons, organize your groups, talk with your colleagues, and grade papers. Your strengths as teachers and your students' strengths as learners will help you connect with the core emotions that first drew you to teaching—your love of kids!

The Strategies

Approaching your teaching with your students' strengths in mind is only the beginning. The teaching focus of our book—literacy strategies for struggling students in mainstream secondary classrooms—is one of many that you can directly impact by an asset approach. Combined with an asset approach to ELLs and linguistic diversity, these research-based strategies are especially effective for students who speak a language other than English at home.

Reading in English is a significant challenge for ELLs because they are trying to make meaning of texts that are written in a language they are still learning. Thus, ELLs need your help. Vocabulary development plays an essential role in comprehension, but it is not the only factor. Struggling students need your help far beyond cracking open new words.

For this reason, in this book, we highlight strategies your students can use before, during, and after reading. Using our strategies in all three phases is important because the essence of comprehension and, indeed, learning in general, often occurs after we read something and are able to apply it in another context. The strategies we focus on first get at the heart of what we call "priming," or eliciting prior knowledge; we then move on to a discussion of during- and after-reading processing strategies. This is the sequence of learning that hr. is particularly effective for ELLs. Traditionally, the connections that public school students make with texts are bound in a cultural context that is both white and English. To become independent readers, students utilize their cultural knowledge to make connections even before they begin reading. This may be as simple as knowing how to use the pictures on the page of a book, or as complex as recognizing satire in an author's tone. These cultural connections are huge assets that white, English-speaking students bring to the classroom.

ELLs typically do not have access to the same cultural and linguistic background knowledge that their mainstream peers possess. You'll be most effective as a teacher if you can help your ELLs make connections with text before they start reading. Additionally, you'll want to help them find meaning from more than just the words of the texts they are reading. This is a challenging task, and we contend that each of the strategies in this book can help you succeed. The priming phase of literacy development takes a lot of time and effort, but it may be the key to our students' success. All students need substantial content knowledge to construct meaning from a text at hand, so you'll want to take your time teaching these strategies, and rely on your students' and your own assessment skills to determine when you can move on. We believe that you will come to appreciate the power of these strategies for all students.

Calling New Teachers

Above all, we hope we've succeeded in helping you believe in yourself as a capable, creative teacher. We urge you to take the time and reconnect with the desires and emotions that brought you into this profession. Let your deepest desires for teaching engagement and success drive your vision for reaching all students.

Spend some time creating and refining your vision of teaching, and determining what teaching really means to you. Although an optimistic teaching vision may not be easy to formulate or maintain, we believe that meeting students where they are and capitalizing on their strengths is a good place to begin. Embracing this asset approach, whether you are a veteran teacher or a brand new one, is crucial because it can help you solidify your ability to empower students—especially those who are accustomed to being labeled "failures" at school. Like all professionals, we teachers need experience to refine our practice. It is our hope that this book will provide our readers with research-based ideas and practices to help frame their teaching vision and put that vision into action in the classroom.

In a word, the asset approach is *healthy*. It is healthy for you as an advocate for your students and public education. It is healthy for your kids, from whom so much is expected every single day during every single class period. And it is a healthy new direction for education in general. The alternative is debilitating. We are currently seeing the deleterious effects of a system that focuses on weaknesses. Fewer students of color are succeeding academically—they aren't finishing high school, they aren't going to college, and they likely aren't embarking on careers that will bring them the sustenance and satisfaction that they deserve (Darling-Hammond, 2007).

The Real Asset

Differentiated instruction is a primary focus in public education today for good reason. It is only by getting to know our students and their unique needs that we will make progress in closing the achievement gap. We have already discussed the growing population of students who speak languages other than English at home, and we have also highlighted the distinctions in academic achievement between Caucasian students and students of color. These are both very important factors in the quest to provide quality instruction for all students. At the heart of the asset approach to ELL instruction is the issue of diversity. Diversity is about differences—in language, experiences, dress, food, learning styles, and opinions. Without diversity, things would be the same—bland, even boring. And it is precisely this that makes diversity such a powerful force in learning.

The seminal case, *Brown v. Board of Education*, established this salient point: everyone benefits from diversity. To this end, this book is not simply about creating equity and overcoming the gap between those students who succeed and those who don't. And it's not just about addressing the unique needs and talents of ELLs or students of color. It is about providing the key literacy strategies *all students* need to succeed, and about the need to start a movement in our public schools that taps the cultural and linguistic resources our students bring to the classroom. The power and wonder of teaching is that every single day, in your own classroom with your own students, you can create and fulfill these opportunities and realize the real promise of education that works for all students.

Appendix A

Group Discussion Log for Sustained Silent Reading Time

Group Members: _____

Period: _____ Date: _____

Book Title and Author: _____

Directions: Answer the following questions about your independent reading book. When you get in your group, these questions will guide your discussion of your book.

1. I chose this book because

2. I would recommend this book to people who like

3. In the space below, provide a brief summary of your book (5 sentences).

Closing the Achievement Gap © 2009 by Noah Borrero and Shawn Bird: Scholastic Professional

Appendix B

Student Interest Survey

Name: _____ Period: _____

Directions: Answer each of the following questions honestly. My goal is to get to know you as a reader and this survey will help me find books that will interest you. It is okay if you can't answer all of the questions, just answer the ones you can.

1. My favorite book is: _____

2. My favorite author is: _____

3. My favorite kind of book is: _____

4. My favorite magazine is: _____

5. My favorite movie is: _____

6. My favorite class in school is: _____

7. What are some of your interests outside of school
   (for example: sports, playing video games):

8. Do you read when you are not in school?

9. If you don't like to read, why not?

10. What would you like me to know about you that will help me
    help you find books you'll enjoy?

Appendix C

Exit Ticket

Name: _____

Period: _____ Date: _____

Two things I learned today that I didn't know before class began:

1. _____

2. _____

Something I have a question about but didn't want to ask out loud:

_____

_____

_____

_____

_____

Closing the Achievement Gap © 2009 by Noah Borrero and Shawn Bird: Scholastic Professional

References

Allen, J. (1995). *It's never too late: Leading adolescents to lifelong literacy*. Portsmouth, New Hampshire: Heinemann.

Alfassi, M. (2004). Reading to learn: Effects of combined strategy instruction on high school students. *Journal of Educational Research, 97(3)*, 171–184.

Anzaldúa, G. (1987). *Borderlands/La frontera*. San Francisco: Aunt Lute Books.

Atwell, N. (2007). *The reading zone: How to help kids become skilled, passionate, habitual, critical readers*. New York: Scholastic.

Bandura, A. (1997). *Self-efficacy: The exercise of control*. New York: W.H. Freeman and Company.

Beers, K. (2003). *When kids can't read: What teachers can do*. Portsmouth, NH: Heinemann.

Benson, P., Leffert, N., Scales, P., & Blyth, D. (1998). Beyond the "village" rhetoric: Creating healthy communities for children and adolescents. *Applied Developmental Science, 2(3)*, 138–159.

Bird, S. (2005). *A content analysis of the most commonly adopted high school literature anthologies*. Unpublished doctoral dissertation, University of Houston.

Borrero, N. (2006). *Promoting academic achievement for bilingual middle school students: Learning strategies for young interpreters*. Unpublished doctoral dissertation, Stanford University.

Borrero, N. (2008). What students see, hear, and do: Linguistic assets at the Bay School. *English Leadership Quarterly, 30 (3)*, 2–5.

Burke, J. (2009) *The teacher's essential guide: Content area reading*. New York: Scholastic.

Butler, Y., & Hakuta, K. (2004). Bilingualism and second language acquisition. In T. Bhatia & W. Ritchie (eds.), *Handbook of bilingualism*. (pp. 114-145). Blackwell Publishers.

Bhatia & W. C. Ritchie (Eds.), *The handbook of bilingualism* (pp. 114–145). Oxford, UK: Blackwell.

Cabrera, N. L., & Padilla, A. M. (2004). Entering and succeeding in the "culture of college": The story of two Mexican heritage students. *Hispanic Journal of Behavioral Sciences, 25*, 1–19.

Camarota, S. A., (2005). Immigrants at mid-decade: A snapshot of America's foreign born population in 2005. Center for immigration studies. Retrieved July 24, 2008, from http://www.cis.org/articles/2005/back1405.html.

Campbell, J. R., Hombo, C., & Mazzeo, J. (2000). *NAEP 1999 Trends in academic progress: Three decades of student performance*. NCES 2000–469. Washington, DC: U.S. Department of Education, National Center for Education Statistics.

Cohen, E., & Lotan, R. (2004). Equity in heterogeneous classrooms. In J. Banks & C. Banks (Eds.). *Handbook of research on multicultural education*. San Francisco: Jossey-Bass.

Crawford, J. (1999). *Bilingual education: History, politics, theory, and practice* (4th ed.). Los Angeles: Bilingual Education Services.

Crawford, J., & Krashen, S. (2007). *English learners in American classrooms*. New York: Scholastic.

Cummins, J. (2000). *Language, power, and pedagogy: Bilingual children in the crossfire*. Buffalo, NY: Multilingual Matters, Ltd.

Cummins, J. (2005). A proposal for action: Strategies for recognizing heritage language competence as a learning resource with the mainstream classroom. In H. Byrnes, (Ed.).

Perspectives. *Modern Language Journal*, 89, iv, 592–616.

Crutcher, C. (2007). *Deadline*. New York: HarperCollins Children's Books.

Darling-Hammond, L. (2007) The flat earth and education: How America's commitment to equity will determine our future. *Educational Researcher*, 36(6), 318-334.

Fountas, I. and Pinnell, G.S. (2006). *Teaching for comprehending and fluency: Thinking, talking, and writing about reading, K–8*. Portsmouth, N.H.: Heinemann.

Freeman, D., & Freeman, Y. (1994). *Between worlds: Access to second language acquisition*. Portsmouth, NH: Heinemann.

Freeman, Y., & Freeman, D. (1998). *ESL/EFL teaching: Principles for success* Portsmouth, NH: Heinemann.

Freeman, D., & Freeman, Y. (2007). *English language learners: The essential guide*. New York: Scholastic.

Gándara, P. (2008). The crisis in the education of Latino students. Civil Rights Project/Proyecto Derechos Civiles, University of California, Los Angeles. Retrieved on July 31, 2008, from http://www.nea.org/achievement/gandara08.html.

Giles, V. (2005). *Secondary school students' (grades 7–12) attitudes toward reading motivational activities*. Unpublished doctoral dissertation, University of Houston.

Goldenberg, C. (2008). Teaching English language learners: What the research does and does not say. *American Educator, 32* (2), 8–23.

Goodman, K. S. (1979). Reading: A psycholinguistic guessing game. In H. Singer & R. B. Ruddell (Eds.). *Theoretical models and processes of reading* (pp. 259-271). Newark, DE: International Reading Association.

Graves, D., & Kittle, P. (2005). *Inside writing: How to teach the details of craft* Portsmouth, NH: Heinemann.

Jackson, Y. (2001). Reversing underachievement in urban students: Pedagogy of confidence. In A. Costa (Ed.). *Developing minds: a resource book for teaching thinking*. Alexandria, VA: ASCD.

Jackson, Y. (2008). Presentation to ASCD Headquarters. Reported in ASCD Smart Brief. Alexandria, VA.: ASCD.

Kamil, M. (2008). *How to get recreational reading to increase reading ability*. In Kim, Y., et al. (Eds.), 57th Yearbook of the National Reading Conference.

Krashen, S. (1982). *Principles and practices in second language acquisition*. Oxford, UK: Pergamon Press.

Krashen, S. (1985). *The input hypothesis: Issues and implications*. New York: Longman.

Krashen, S. (1999). *Condemned without a trial: Bogus arguments against bilingual education*. Portsmouth, NH: Heinemann.

Krashen, S. (2004). *The power of reading: Insights from the research*. Portsmouth, NH: Heinemann.

Kubota, R. (2005). Second language teaching for multilingual and multiculturalism: Politics, challenges, and possibilities. In R. Hoosain. & F. Salili (Eds.). *Language in multicultural education (pp. 31–55)*. Connecticut: Information Age Publishing.

Laminack, L. (2009). *Unwrapping the read aloud: Making every read aloud intentional and instructional*. New York: Scholastic.

Lewis, A. (2003). Everyday race-making. *The American Behavioral Scientist; 47* (3): 283–305.

Livaudais, M. (1985). *A survey of secondary (grades 7–12) students' attitudes toward reading motivational activities*. Unpublished doctoral dissertation, University of *Houston*.

Lyman, F. (1981). The responsive classroom discussion: The inclusion of all students. In A. Anderson (Ed.). *Mainstreaming Digest (pp. 109–113)*. College Park, MD: University of Maryland College of Education.

Mackey, W. F. (1957). The description of bilingualism. *Journal of the Canadian Linguistic Association (7, 51–85)*.

Malakoff, M., & Hakuta, K. (1991). Translation skill and metalinguistic awareness in bilinguals. In E. Bialystok (Ed.), *Language processing in bilingual children* (pp. 141-166). Cambridge: Cambridge University Press.

Martinez, E. (1998). Seeing more than black and white. *De colores means all of us: Latina views for a multi-colored century*. Cambridge: South End Press.

McTighe, J., & Lyman, F. T. (1988). Cueing thinking in the classroom: The promise of theory-embedded tools. *Educational Leadership, 45* (7), 18–24.

Modern Language Association. (2005). The modern language association language map: A map of languages in the United States. Retrieved July 24, 2008, from http://www.mla.org/map_data.

Moll, L. C., Amanti, C., Neff, D., & González, N. (1992). Funds of knowledge for teaching: Using a qualitative approach to connect homes and classrooms. *Theory into Practice*, 31(2): 132–141.

Morales, A., & Hanson, W. E. (2005). Language brokering: an integrative review of the literature. *Hispanic Journal of Behavioral Sciences*, 27, 471–503.

National Center for Education Statistics. (2005). NAEP trends in student groups. U.S. Department of Education, National Assessment of Educational Progress. Retrieved July 31, 2008, from http://nces.ed.gov.

Nessel, D. D., & Graham, J. M. (2007). *Thinking strategies for student achievement* Thousand Oaks, CA: Corwin.

Nichols, M. (2009). *Expanding comprehension with multigenre text sets*. New York: Scholastic.

Nieto, S. (2002). *Language, culture, and teaching: Critical perspectives for a new century*. Mahwah, NJ: Lawrence Erlbaum Associates, Inc.

Olsen, L. (1997). *Made in America: Immigrant students in our public schools*. New York: New Press: Distributed by W.W. Norton.

Ovando, C. J., Combs, M. C., & Collier, V. P. (2006). *Bilingual & ESL classrooms: Teaching in multicultural contexts* (4th ed.). Boston: McGraw Hill.

Padilla, A. (2006). Second language learning: Issues in research and teaching. In P. A. Alexander, P. R. Pintrich, & P. H. Winne (Eds.), *Handbook of educational psychology (pp. 571–591)*. New York: Erlbaum Association.

Palinscar, A. S. & Brown, A. L. (1984). Reciprocal teaching of comprehension-fostering and comprehension-monitoring activities. *Cognition and Instruction (1,117–175)*.

Pilgreen, J. (2000). The SSR handbook: How to organize and manage a sustained silent reading program. Portsmouth, New Hampshire: Heinemann.

Portes, A., & Rumbaut, R. G. (2001). Legacies: The story of the immigrant second generation. Berkeley, CA: University of California Press.

Ray, K.W. (2006). *Study driven: A framework for planning units of study in the writing workshop*. Portsmouth, New Hampshire: Heinemann.

Rickford, J. R., & Rickford, R. J. (2000). *Spoken soul: The story of black English*. New York: John Wiley & Sons, Inc.

Serafini, F. & Giorgis, C. (2003). *Reading aloud and beyond: Fostering the intellectual life with older readers*. Portsmouth, NH: Heinemann.

Short, D., & Fitzsimmons, S. (2007). *Double the work: Challenges and solutions to acquiring language and academic literacy for adolescent English language learners—A report to Carnegie Corporation of New York*. Washington, DC: Alliance for Excellent Education.

Short, J., Echevarria, J., & Vogt, M. (2004). *Making content comprehensible for English learners: The SIOP model*. Boston: Allyn and Bacon.

Smith, F. (1988). *Joining the literacy club: Further essays into education*. Portsmouth, NH: Heinemann.

(1982). *Writing and the writer*. Hillsdale, NJ: Lawrence Earlbaum Associates.

Steele, C. (2004). A threat in the air. In J. Banks. & C. Banks. (Eds.) *Handbook of research on multicultural education*. San Francisco: Jossey-Bass.

Suarez-Orozco, M., & Suarez-Orozco, C. (2001). *Children of immigration*. Cambridge, MA: Harvard University Press.

Tatum, B. (2003). *Why are all the black kids sitting together in the cafeteria?* New York: Basic Books.

Tomlinson, C. A. (2001). *How to differentiate instruction in mixed-ability classrooms*. Alexandria, VA: ASCD.

Tovani, C. (2001). *I read it but I don't get it: Comprehension strategies for adolescent readers*. Portland, ME: Stenhouse Publishers.

Tovani, C. (2004). *Do I really have to teach reading? Content comprehension, grades 6–12*. Portland, ME: Stenhouse Publishers.

Trelease, J. (2001). *The read-aloud handbook*. New York, Penguin.

Trelease, J. (2006). *The read-aloud handbook*. New York: Penguin.

Tse, L. (1995). Language brokering among Latino adolescents: Prevalence, attitudes, and school performance. *Hispanic Journal of Behavioral Sciences, 17*, (2), 180–193.

Tse, L. (1996). Who decides? The effects of language brokering on home-school communication. *The Journal of Educational Issues of Language Minority Students, 16*, 225–234.

Turner, A. (2008, June, 9). Cancer patient had salmonella prior to death. the *Houston Chronicle*, p. A-2.

Vacca, R., & Vacca, J. (2005). *Content area reading: Literacy and learning across the curriculum*, 8th ed. Boston: Allyn & Bacon.

Valdés, G. (2001) *Learning and not learning English: Latino students in American schools*. New York, NY: Teachers College Press.

Valdés, G. (2003). *Expanding definitions of giftedness: Young interpreters of immigrant background*. New Jersey: Erlbaum.

Weisskirch, R. S. (2005). The relationship of language brokering to ethnic identity for Latino early adolescents. *Hispanic Journal of Behavioral Sciences, 27*, 286-289.

Wilhelm, J., Baker, T., & Dube, J. (2001). *Strategic reading: Guiding students to lifelong literacy, 6–12*. Portsmouth, NH: Heinemann.

Wu, F. H. (2001). Model minority: Asian American "success" as race relations failure. In *Yellow* (pp. 39–78). New York: Basic Books.

Index